Marks of a Healthy Church

D0974281

Marks of a Healthy Church

by
John MacArthur, Jr.

"GRACE TO YOU"
P.O. Box 4000
Panorama City, CA   91412

© 1990 by
JOHN F. MACARTHUR, JR.

All rights reserved. No part of this book may be reproduced in any form without permission in writing from the publisher, except in the case of brief quotations embodied in critical articles or reviews.

All Scripture quotations, unless noted otherwise, are from the *New Scofield Reference Bible*, King James Version. Copyright © 1967 by Oxford University Press, Inc. Reprinted by permission.

ISBN: 0-8024-5338-4

1 2 3 4 5 6 Printing/LC/Year 94 93 92 91 90

Printed in the United States of America

Contents

These Bible studies are taken from messages delivered by Pastor-Teacher John MacArthur, Jr., at Grace Community Church in Panorama City, California. These messages have been combined into a 8-tape album titled *Marks of a Healthy Church*. You may purchase this series either in an attractive vinyl cassette album or as individual cassettes. To purchase these tapes, request the album *Marks of a Healthy Church*, or ask for the tapes by their individual GC numbers. Please consult the current price list; then, send your order, making your check payable to:

The Master's Communication
P.O. Box 4000
Panorama City, CA 91412

Or call the following toll-free number:
1-800-55-GRACE

1
Marks of an Effective Church—Part 1

Outline

Introduction
  A. The Sovereign Choice of God
  B. The Suggested Reasons for Growth

Lesson
 I. Godly Leaders
  A. The General Requirement
  B. The Specific Requirements
 II. Functional Goals and Objectives
  A. Recognizing Biblical Goals
  B. Responding to God's Direction
III. Discipleship
  A. Determining the Church's Responsibility
  B. Delineating the Discipling Process
    1. Teach biblical truth
    2. Apply Scripture to life
    3. Solve problems biblically
IV. Penetrating the Community
  A. The Model of the Early Church
    1. Inside Jerusalem
    2. Outside Jerusalem
  B. The Methods of the Modern Church
    1. The program approach
      a) Exemplified
      b) Evaluated
    2. The personal approach
 V. Active Church Members

Introduction

I have a great love for the church—not only for Grace Community Church but for the church of our Lord Jesus Christ as a whole. I also have a great love for pastors and a desire for us to shape our churches into what God wants them to be. When I recall the apostle Paul's instruction to take care of the church that Christ "purchased with his own blood" (Acts 20:28), I am sobered by that tremendous responsibility.

The congregation of the church I pastor endeavors to be obedient to the Word of God. Although we are not all that God would have us be, we believe we have a grip on some of the basics that make a church what it ought to be. We are often approached by the leadership of other churches asking us for help. They want to know why God has blessed us.

A. The Sovereign Choice of God

> God has displayed proof of His power and presence again and again at our church. We've seen people saved, lives changed, and families restored. Christians are maturing. And people come from many places to be a part of Grace church. God is doing marvelous things in our midst, and it may be only a preview of what He will yet do, should He tarry. People want to know why God has blessed us with such dynamic ministries. Others teach the same Scripture, look to the same Holy Spirit, and worship the same Lord; but they don't get the same results. Why not?

> Perhaps the best answer is that God has sovereignly chosen to accomplish what He will at our church—we are only spectators. Although He works through men and women, Christ continues to build His church His way, in spite of what we do (cf. Matt: 16:18). But beyond His sovereign work, we must submit to certain principles that will allow any church to be what the Lord wants it to be.

B. The Suggested Reasons for Growth

> Size is not a factor to consider in analyzing the success of a church. Some churches God blesses are very small, whereas some that are very large have little or no spiritual fruit.

A church's spiritual life cannot be measured by its numbers. It is easy to attract people, but it is far more difficult to make disciples. Yet it appears as though churches across America are in a contest to build the biggest church. In fact, conferences are held across our nation to teach people how to do that. I've never gone to one, and I don't intend to. Size is irrelevant to God.

Lesson

There are reasons a church prospers spiritually that are important for us to understand. The following are key ingredients of a church that is successful by God's standards:

I. GODLY LEADERS

A. The General Requirement

You cannot ignore the necessity of having godly leadership and still receive God's blessing. Holy men and women must be in positions of responsibility in a church. Paul repeatedly said that Christ is the head of the church (1 Cor. 11:3; Eph. 1:22; 4:15; 5:23; Col. 1:18). As its head, Christ wants to rule His church through holy people. Unholy people get in the way.

It is amazing how many churches choose their leadership. They select people who are the most successful in business, who have the most to say, and who have the most money. A pastor confessed to me that one of the problems he had in working with his board was that half of them were not Christians. That is a serious problem because Satan and Christ don't cooperate! A man is not to be a leader in the church because he is the best businessman, has innate leadership ability, or is a super-salesman. He should be a leader because he is a man of God.

God has always mediated His rule in the world through godly people. In the beginning, God mediated His rule through Adam. After the Fall, He mediated through human conscience. After the Flood, it was through government. Eventually God began to mediate His rule through the patriarchs, the judges, and then the kings, prophets, and priests. In the gospel accounts He ruled through Christ. And now He rules through the church, whose leaders are representatives of Jesus Christ in the world.

The primary ingredient in church leadership is holiness. However, it takes time to develop holy leadership. It took God forty years to make Moses into the leader He wanted. Joshua was an understudy of Moses for years before he was ready to lead the Israelites into the Promised Land. It took years as well to prepare Abraham and David. It took time to get Peter, Philip, and Paul ready for their far-reaching ministries. It takes time to make a man of God.

B. The Specific Requirements

When Timothy stayed in Ephesus, he had the responsibility of bringing the church to spiritual maturity. He knew he couldn't do it alone and that he needed godly leaders. Paul had told him it was commendable for a man to desire to be a leader in the church—as long as he was the right kind of man. A church shouldn't accept just any volunteers; it should look for godly men. Titus faced the same challenge in Crete, and Paul gave him similar advice. In 1 Timothy 3:1-7 and Titus 1:5-9 Paul gives a profile of the kind of people that are to be leading the church. They are to be:

1. Above reproach (1 Tim. 3:2)—Leaders are to be blameless, having nothing in their lives for which they can be rebuked.

2. Devoted to their wives (1 Tim. 3:2)—They are to be one-woman men.

3. Temperate (1 Tim. 3:2)—They are to be spiritually stable, having a clear, biblical perspective on life.

4. Prudent (1 Tim. 3:2)—They are to be sober-minded, knowing their priorities.

5. Respectable (1 Tim. 3:2)—Leaders are to have such well-ordered lives that they are honored for it.

6. Hospitable (1 Tim. 3:2)—They are to love strangers, opening their homes to those in need.

7. Able to teach (1 Tim. 3:2)—That phrase is translated from the single Greek word *didaktikos*. It is never used to speak of the gift of teaching or the office of a teacher. It is not saying every leader must be a great Bible teacher. It is saying he must be teachable and able to communicate biblical truth to others. The word conveys not so much the dynamics of his teaching as his sensitivity to others. He teaches with a meek and gentle spirit.

8. Self-controlled (Titus 1:8)—Leaders are not to be addicted to alcohol or drugs of any kind. They need to exercise self-control.

9. Not self-willed (Titus 1:7)—They should not be self-centered. A church can't have people in leadership who are concerned only about themselves. The most important thing about church leaders is that they be concerned about the people they are shepherding.

10. Not quick-tempered (Titus 1:7)—Those in leadership cannot have a volatile temperament; they must be patient.

11. Not pugnacious (Titus 1:7)—This literally means "not a fighter." A church doesn't want someone in leadership who solves problems with his fists.

12. Not contentious (1 Tim. 3:3)—This attitude corresponds to the previous physical reaction. A contentious person likes to compete and debate.

13. Gentle (1 Tim. 3:3)

14. Not materialistic (1 Tim. 3:3)—Church leaders must be free from the love of money (but that is not to say they should be free from money itself).

15. Good managers of their households (1 Tim. 3:4)—Church leaders are required to keep their children un-

der control, with dignity. Many people keep their kids under control, but not many do it with dignity.

16. Of good repute among unbelievers (1 Tim. 3:7)—What does the world think of church leaders? As they interact with the unsaved world, their integrity should be above reproach.

17. Lovers of good (Titus 1:8)

18. Just (Titus 1:8)—Church leaders are to be fair.

19. Devout (Titus 1:8)—They must also be holy in their daily lives.

20. Not new converts (1 Tim. 3:6)—They are to be spiritually mature.

Those are the qualifications given in Scripture for leaders in the church. They indicate the kind of people God wants to lead His church. If a church doesn't have people who measure up to God's standards, there will be problems at the very beginning. In fact, godly leadership is so important that when an elder sins, he is to be rebuked before the whole congregation (1 Tim. 5:20).

To Flee or to Follow?

From a negative perspective, Paul told Timothy that the "man of God" must flee pride, materialism, discontentment, and disputes (1 Tim. 6:11). But on the positive side, he is to follow after righteousness, godliness, faith, love, patience, and meekness as he fights the good fight of faith (vv. 11-12). In the leadership of the church there must be many godly men.

II. FUNCTIONAL GOALS AND OBJECTIVES

A church must have functional goals and objectives, or it will have no direction. A church that lacks direction will have no sense of accomplishment. We cannot be like the man who jumped on his horse and rode off madly in all directions! There must be some direction to what we're trying to accomplish. Can you imagine a baseball game with no bases? After hitting the ball, you wouldn't know what to do. People need goals and clear-cut objectives. It has been well said that the reason so many of us feel we're doing so well is that we don't know what we're doing!

A. Recognizing Biblical Goals

We must first recognize the basic biblical goals of the church: to win people to Christ and to help them mature. Beneath those overarching goals are more specific ones, such as unifying families, preventing divorce, and educating children in the things of the Lord. Those are just a few of the many biblical goals we have.

In addition, we must have functional objectives. Those are the stepping stones we use to accomplish biblical goals. It isn't enough to say we must learn the Word of God. We must go a step further and provide steps to attain that goal. For example, if we want to win people to Christ, we might preach about the responsibility of the believer to evangelize, and offer classes in evangelism.

B. Responding to God's Direction

Some goals and objectives we set are never fulfilled because God has different plans. Proverbs 16:9 says, "The mind of man plans his way, but the Lord directs his steps" (NASB*). It is God's prerogative to divert us from our plans.

In Acts 16 the apostle Paul was trying to enter Bithynia, having already been forbidden by the Holy Spirit to speak in Asia. But the Spirit didn't let him speak in Bithynia either. Prevented from going north or south and already having been east, Paul headed west. Then he received a vision confirming his decision to continue west to Macedonia (vv. 6-10).

Later in his ministry, Paul wrote to the Roman Christians, saying he would visit them on his way to Spain (Rom.

* *New American Standard Bible.*

15:28). We don't know if he ever got to Spain, but at least that was his goal. Some goals and objectives are realized and some aren't, but all of them must be submitted to the Lord's direction.

Functional goals and objectives are essential. A church can't be nebulous in its direction. The people must know where they are going and how to get there.

III. DISCIPLESHIP

A. Determining the Church's Responsibility

A church must make a concerted effort to teach people the Word of God to bring them to maturity. Everyone is to be involved in that process: the teaching pastor is to perfect the saints, and the saints are to do the work of the ministry so that the Body of Christ may be built up. We are all to be involved in the process of discipling people. Paul instructed Timothy to pass on what he had learned to faithful men who would "be able to teach others also" (2 Tim. 2:2). Older men and women are to teach the younger ones (Titus 2:3-5). Even young men are to be examples to others (Titus 2:6-7). A Christian who isn't discipling someone is a contradiction. He ought to be reproducing his life in the lives of others.

A church should emphasize discipleship. The design of the Christian church is not to have a professional preacher financed by laymen who merely act as spectators. Every Christian should be involved in edifying other believers.

Someone once asked me when I did my pastoral visitation. Many pastors "do visitation" in the afternoons after studying in the morning. But where does the Bible say that a pastor is to visit others all afternoon? One of the few things it does say about visitation is found in the book of James: "Pure religion and undefiled before God and the Father is this: to visit the fatherless and widows in their affliction" (1:27). Who is to be involved in pure and undefiled religion? Is it just the preacher? No. Every Christian is. If you have someone to visit, do so. If I know someone who needs to be visited, I must do the same. There is no sense

14

in my visiting those whom you ought to visit, and in your visiting those whom I ought to visit. As a pastor, I don't believe I am called to be the official visitor. Visitation—and the related ministry of discipleship—is everyone's responsibility.

B. Delineating the Discipling Process

1. Teach biblical truth

The Greek word translated "disciple" (*mathētēs*) means "learner." If someone is a learner, someone else must teach him. Discipling Christians means teaching them biblical truth. When I disciple people, I give them books to read and tapes to listen to that deal with biblical topics they need to understand. Besides teaching from the pulpit, I teach them biblical truths on a personal level from the Word of God.

2. Apply Scripture to life

You need to make the Bible come alive to the person you're discipling by making it practical. He must know how to apply biblical truth. You would be amazed at how many people learn principles that they never put into action. I ask questions that prompt the disciple to think through his own set of circumstances from God's perspective. I want him to interpret life spiritually. For example, a man I was discipling was panicking over the world situation. But as he began viewing the world from the standpoint of a sovereign God and not from that of a desperate human, his panic disappeared. Then he became excited to see what God was doing in the world. Biblical truth must be taught and then translated into appropriate attitudes and actions.

3. Solve problems biblically

Biblical problem solving is a key to effective discipleship. People learn best when they have a need to know. One example is the way people respond to the stewardess giving safety instructions before takeoff. No one pays any attention to her—except those who are on

15

their first flight—because they've heard it all before and don't expect to need to know it. However, if you looked out the right side of the plane and saw flames coming from the engine just as the stewardess said, "Please take your emergency card," you would grab one of those cards. And if there weren't enough cards for everyone, someone would get trampled trying to find one! The change in interest level comes from suddenly needing to know.

You always learn best when you *have* to know the answers. Effective discipleship involves giving someone biblical answers to problems he has and teaching him how to apply those answers. You can't just lecture; you've got to know enough Scripture to give your disciple answers when he needs them.

You may think you don't know much. Yet there are bound to be people who don't know as much as you do. Find one of them and begin to disciple him. It is an unparalleled joy to see your disciples mature and grow. A Christian ought to be sharing the life he has received from God with others.

IV. PENETRATING THE COMMUNITY

A church that is effective and successful will have a strong emphasis on penetrating the community. The Bible makes clear that we're to reach people for Christ.

A. The Model of the Early Church

1. Inside Jerusalem

In the first few chapters of Acts we see that the early church blitzed their community. On the Day of Pentecost, three thousand people were saved. In turn those people moved through Jerusalem like wildfire. That church grew so fast that the Jewish leaders said to the apostles, "Ye have filled Jerusalem with your doctrine" (5:28). Their message had penetrated the entire community.

No One Gets to Heaven by Watching a Christian

The nearest many Christians come to penetrating their community is driving to church in a car that has a fish sticker on the back window! We come to church and say, "I've done my duty to God." We try to live our testimony rather than speak it. But no one ever got to heaven just because he watched someone live his testimony in front of him. Sooner or later you've got to explain the gospel.

2. Outside Jerusalem

   The early Christians didn't isolate themselves in a corner and talk about doctrine. They went out and saturated their communities with the gospel.

   a) Acts 13:44—"The next sabbath day came almost the whole city together to hear the word of God." The Christians of Antioch were so busy that when it came time for preaching, nearly the whole city showed up. That was typical of the early church.

   b) Acts 14:1—"It came to pass in Iconium that they went both together into the synagogue of the Jews, and so spoke, that a great multitude, both of the Jews and also of the Greeks, believed." Paul and Barnabas confronted both Jews and Gentiles with the gospel.

   c) Acts 16:5—Paul, Silas, and Timothy established the churches of Phrygia and Galatia "in the faith, and [they] increased in number daily."

   d) Acts 17:3-4—Paul entered into the Thessalonian synagogue, "opening and alleging that Christ must needs have suffered, and risen again from the dead. . . . And some of them believed . . . and of the devout Greeks a great multitude [believed]." They proclaimed the truth to their community, and the people responded. That is characteristic of every successful church throughout history.

B. The Methods of the Modern Church

A church can reach the community in several ways.

1. The program approach

   a) Exemplified

   Some people go wild on programs of evangelism. I attended a banquet where a church was presenting its evangelistic program for the year. It was centered around a football theme. A scoreboard and goal posts were set up in the auditorium. When anyone got saved, they kicked the ball through the goal posts! Furthermore, to motivate people to evangelize, five footballs were hidden in the homes of five unsaved families. Whoever found a football won a prize. The church also set up a hot dog stand. They even gave out sweaters to the kids who brought a certain number of people to church. I couldn't believe all the gimmicks they were using!

   b) Evaluated

   I can't help but think that giving people ulterior motives for winning someone to the Lord is the worst possible way to evangelize. Consider the feelings of the unsaved people who were brought to church so that church members could win prizes!

   After that incredible event, I was asked to speak to a group of pastors about the biblical directives for the church. I used the football program as an illustration of what not to do in evangelism. As I spoke, I noticed that there wasn't much reaction. Several days later, I received a letter from the pastor of the church that had held the evangelism banquet. It said: "Dear Rev. MacArthur, I suppose if you had known that I had been in that class, you wouldn't have said what you said about our program. Secondly, I know you wouldn't have said it had you known that the hour before, I had presented the program to the same group of pastors you spoke to." My heart started beating faster when I read that! I immediately called him to confirm my love for him and to apologize for offending him. However, I also told him that I still stood 100 percent behind what I had said and that I wouldn't change my opinion of that kind of program.

2. The personal approach

The church doesn't need manipulative programs. If you try to motivate people to do things for selfish motives, their actions will not honor God. I'm not against visitation nights or door-to-door evangelism, but the best way to penetrate the community is to have Christians who reproduce themselves in their everyday lives. Then you don't need programs. Which would you rather have: a week of revival meetings once a year or a congregation evangelizing 365 days a year? Obviously the latter. Evangelism ought to be going on all the time. And it is important that we do it on a personal level.

V. ACTIVE CHURCH MEMBERS

Something is wrong with a church in which the staff does everything. The pastoral staff should equip the saints to do the work of the ministry (Eph. 4:12). The ministry of the church extends to all believers. Romans 12:6-8 delineates some of the different spiritual gifts God has given Christians to use in the church: "Having then gifts differing according to the grace that is given to us, whether prophecy, let us prophesy according to the proportion of faith; or ministry, let us wait on our ministering; or he that teacheth, on teaching; or he that exhorteth, on exhortation; he that giveth, let him do it with liberality; he that ruleth, with diligence; he that showeth mercy, with cheerfulness." Until the church realizes that every member must minister his gifts, it never will be what God wants it to be.

Baseball pitcher Dizzy Dean's career ended when his toe was hit by a line drive. That injury ruined his throwing motion because when he came off the rubber to pitch, he had to compensate by turning his foot the wrong way. Consequently he began overextending his arm, which eventually ruined it for pitching. That same principle is true in the church. Where there are nonfunctioning members, there will be adverse effects somewhere else in the Body. All the saints must be involved in ministering the gifts God has given them.

We don't want to recruit people to run programs; we want to mature saints who will do their ministries. I've talked to many pastors who are discouraged because their programs keep falling apart. I decided a long time ago that I wouldn't promote programs; I want to help the saints mature so that they can develop their own programs. Then they will have the internal motivation necessary to carry them out.

When people in my church say to me, "We need such-and-such a program in our church," I say, "Good, if you feel that way, go ahead and do it." After I had been giving that response for a few years, no one asked about starting a program unless he or she was very serious. The church should emphasize that every individual believer needs to minister. Church leadership shouldn't try to force their members to do something they aren't motivated or gifted to do. Rather, the leadership should develop its members along the lines in which the Spirit has gifted them. Aggressive, active, ministering people make for a successful church.

Focusing on the Facts

1. Why can't a church's spiritual growth be measured by the number of people who attend it (see pp. 8-9)?
2. What basic principle must a church follow to receive God's blessing (see p. 9)?
3. Unfortunately, how do many churches choose their leadership? Why would a mixed group of saved and unsaved church leaders make a church ineffective (see p. 9)?
4. How has God mediated His rule on earth in the past? How has He chosen to rule now (see pp. 9-10)?
5. What was Timothy's responsibility in Ephesus? How was he to accomplish that (see p. 10)?
6. Explain what it means for a church leader to be able to teach (1 Tim. 3:2; see p. 11).
7. Why must a church have functional goals and objectives (see pp. 11-13)?
8. Identify the two basic biblical goals of the church. How do biblical goals relate to functional objectives (see p. 13)?

9. Assuming that we do everything in our power to accomplish our objectives, how can we be prevented from realizing their fulfillment? Give an example from Scripture (see pp. 13-14).
10. Who is to be involved in the process of bringing young Christians to spiritual maturity? Explain (see p. 14).
11. What are three essential elements in the process of discipling others? Describe how to do each one (see pp. 15-16).
12. What happened as the Jerusalem church penetrated the community after the Day of Pentecost (see p. 16)?
13. What two methods of penetrating the community are used by the church today? Which one is preferred? Why (see pp. 18-19)?
14. According to Ephesians 4:12, what is a church's pastoral staff responsible to do (see p. 19)?
15. What happens when members of a church do not minister their gifts to the rest of the Body (see p. 19)?
16. When will church members have the internal motivation to carry out a program (see p. 20)?

Pondering the Principles

1. Although you may not presently be a leader in your church, you should still be following the same advice Paul gave to Timothy. Read 1 Timothy 6:3-12. What things should you be fleeing from? Are there some bad habits or ungodly attitudes you should eliminate through the cleansing power of the Word and the Holy Spirit? Concentrate on pursuing "righteousness, godliness, faith, love, patience, [and] meekness" (v. 11).

2. Proverbs 16:9 says, "The mind of man plans his way, but the Lord directs his steps" (NASB). Do you make unilateral decisions apart from the guidance of the Holy Spirit? Have you made plans that don't seem to be coming to pass as you had expected? Could it be that the Lord is redirecting your steps for a reason that is not yet clear to you? The Lord said, "My thoughts are not your thoughts, neither are your ways my ways, saith the Lord. For as the heavens are higher than the earth, so are my ways higher than your ways, and my thoughts than your thoughts" (Isa. 55:8-9). Praise the Lord that He is infinitely wiser than we are and that He will accomplish His will in our lives as we yield ourselves to His control.

3. If you are not already discipling someone, try to identify a Christian in your sphere of influence who could benefit from your spiritual maturity. Are you willing to share your life with that person as you teach him or her how to solve problems biblically? Since learning takes place best when there is a need to know, you will need to be available in crisis situations. Discipling someone isn't easy, but the joy and sense of accomplishment it brings are more than worth the effort.

4. How are you penetrating your community? Is your evangelism limited to a bumper sticker on your car or your moral life-style? There are many people who don't know Christ yet lead moral lives. Godly living is important in evangelism, but it isn't enough. Words that confront unbelief and explain the need for divine forgiveness must follow your godly actions. You need to communicate the simple gospel truths that were necessary for you to come to faith in Christ. If you want to know more about effectively communicating your faith, read some books on evangelism or take an evangelism training class. The best education, however, takes place in your daily life as you share the gospel. Pray for sensitivity to the opportunities God brings to you this week.

2
Marks of an Effective Church—Part 2

Outline

Review
 I. Godly Leaders
 II. Functional Goals and Objectives
 III. Discipleship
 IV. Penetrating the Community
 V. Active Church Members

Lesson
 VI. Concern for One Another
　　A. Stated
　　B. Supported
　　　　1. By the epistles
　　　　2. By the Lord
　　　　　　a) The man oppressed with demons
　　　　　　b) The woman afflicted with hemorrhaging
　　　　　　c) The woman caught in adultery
 VII. Devotion to the Family
　　A. The Trend in the Modern Church
　　B. The Testimony of the Word of God
　　　　1. The command to honor your parents
　　　　2. The consequences for dishonoring your parents
　　　　　　a) Stated
　　　　　　b) Illustrated
 VIII. Bible Teaching and Preaching
　　A. The Focal Point
　　B. The False Priorities
　　　　1. No preaching
　　　　2. Positive preaching
　　　　3. Problem preaching

IX. A Willingness to Change
   A. The Issues of Change vs. Tradition
      1. The times of worship
      2. The place of worship
   B. The Illustration of Change vs. Tradition
      1. The context
      2. The confusion
      3. The contrast
      4. The condemnation
X. Great Faith
   A. Exemplified
   B. Exhorted
XI. Sacrifice
XII. Worshiping God

Conclusion

Review

Many kinds of churches exist in a variety of cultures. They minister in many ways through different gifts and offices. For that reason all churches need not conform to the same patterns or use the same methods. However, some common denominators are true of every successful and effective church. They may be administered in different ways and accomplished through different means, but those elements must be present.

Not all successful churches have every factor. But every church has some of them. The more they have, the more dynamic they are. We see those factors not only supported by Scripture but also validated by effective churches in which they are implemented.

I. GODLY LEADERS (see pp. 9-12)

II. FUNCTIONAL GOALS AND OBJECTIVES (see pp. 12-14)

III. DISCIPLESHIP (see pp. 14-16)

IV. PENETRATING THE COMMUNITY (see pp. 16-19)

V. ACTIVE CHURCH MEMBERS (see pp. 19-21)

Lesson

VI. CONCERN FOR ONE ANOTHER

A. Stated

A dynamic church will be involved in the lives of its people. Many churches are simply places where people go to watch things happen. But the church cannot sit in stagnation. Its members cannot merely come in, sit down, walk out, and say that they are involved in what the church is doing. The New Testament is full of exhortations about ministering our spiritual gifts and responding appropriately to others. We have a tremendous responsibility to serve one another.

Why Go to Church?

I was listening to a radio preacher scream at the top of his voice. He was in one of those "amen" congregations where you can hardly hear the preacher for the people's shouting back. For several minutes he kept saying, "When I was a boy, I remember when people went to church. What we need to do is go to church—we need to get back to church." But those people were already in church. They didn't need to hear that. What he really needed to do was tell them why they were there.

We've heard other people say that America needs to get back to church. However, America never understood what it was supposed to do there, so people stopped going. Now we want people to go back, but we're still not telling them what to do when they get there.

Why do we go to church? Hebrews 10:24-25 says, "Let us consider one another to provoke unto love and to good works, not forsaking the assembling of ourselves together, as the manner of some is, but exhorting one another." We don't attend church just to listen. We should be encouraging one another to do good. Every Christian ought to be like a battery that joins with other believers and corporately increases the church's output.

B. Supported

The New Testament has much to say about how believers respond to one another. Concern toward others is an important theme in Scripture.

1. By the epistles

   a) James 5:16—We are to confess our sins one to another.

   b) Colossians 3:13—We are to forgive one another.

   c) Galatians 6:2—We are to bear one another's burdens.

   d) Titus 1:13—We are to rebuke one another.

   e) 1 Thessalonians 4:18—We are to comfort one another.

   f) Hebrews 10:25—We are to exhort one another.

   g) Romans 14:19—We are to edify one another.

   h) Romans 15:14—We are to admonish one another, which means counseling with a view toward changing behavior.

   i) James 5:16—We are to pray for one another.

   All those *one anothers* clearly indicate the responsibilities that Christians have toward each other.

2. By the Lord

   Our Lord Jesus Christ was involved with individuals. He was a caring, sensitive, loving friend who personally interacted with the lives of others. He brought joy to a wedding. He associated with drunkards who needed help, even to the extent that people started calling Him one, too. He met with weak and unimportant people and made them eternally important. He met with perverse and hostile people and revealed a warmth that made Him approachable.

a) The man oppressed with demons

When Jesus arrived in the country of the Gadarenes near the Sea of Galilee, He was met by a madman who "cried with a loud voice, and said, What have I to do with thee, Jesus, thou Son of the Most High God?" (Mark 5:7). The man was demon-possessed. He "had his dwelling among the tombs; and no man could bind him, no, not with chains; for he had been often bound with fetters and chains, and the chains had been plucked asunder by him, and the fetters broken in pieces; neither could any man tame him" (vv. 3-4). Obviously people avoided him! But Jesus took care of him. After Jesus cast the demon out, the villagers found the man "sitting, and clothed, and in his right mind" (v. 15). Jesus got involved in that man's life and transformed it.

b) The woman afflicted with hemorrhaging

As Jesus was walking amid a crowd of people pressing around Him, a woman grabbed one of the tassels on His robe, hoping to be healed (Mark 5:24-29). "Jesus, immediately knowing in himself that power had gone out of him, turned about in the crowd, and said, Who touched my clothes? And his disciples said unto him, Thou seest the multitude crowding thee, and sayest thou, Who touched me?" (vv. 30-31). But Jesus identified the woman and graciously healed her (v. 34).

c) The woman caught in adultery

Some scribes and Pharisees caught a woman in the act of adultery and brought her to Jesus. They hoped to accuse Jesus of undermining the law of

Moses (John 8:3-6), but He "stooped down, and with his finger wrote on the ground, as though he heard them not. So when they continued asking him, he lifted himself up, and said unto them, He that is without sin among you, let him first cast a stone at her" (vv. 6-7). Without condemning her, Jesus told her to "go, and sin no more" (v. 11).

The church must be a loving community that shares with one another. Often we think we've done our job if we've gone to church—where we sit down, listen, get back in the car, and go about our business. God help us if that's our perspective of what a church is.

VII. DEVOTION TO THE FAMILY

A. The Trend in the Modern Church

There was a time when the family functioned as a unit. Every member went to church together and sat in the same pew every Sunday. But as the church became program-oriented, everyone went off and did his own thing. Groups were formed to counteract the loss of identity in our rapidly growing technological society. Older people became known as "senior citizens." Children identified with youth groups that, in many cases, set the pace for the rest of the church. Soon the church began to leave the parents behind. However, the emphasis needs to be balanced among all family members.

B. The Testimony of the Word of God

The importance of the family is stressed many places in Scripture.

1. The command to honor your parents

Exodus 20:12 records the fifth of the Ten Commandments: "Honor thy father and thy mother, that thy days may be long upon the land which the Lord thy God giveth thee."

2. The consequences for dishonoring your parents

   a) Stated

      (1) Exodus 21:15, 17

         The consequences of dishonoring one's parents give us an idea of how serious God is about the matter: "He that smiteth his father, or his mother, shall be surely put to death" (v. 15). I'll never forget seeing a friend of mine punch his father so hard that he knocked him into a bathtub. Some people might think that's funny, but God doesn't. Such an action would have been cause for capital punishment in the Old Testament. Many of you may never hit your father or mother, but do you think evil thoughts about them or curse them? Verse 17 says, "He that curseth his father, or his mother, shall surely be put to death." Execution was God's punishment for such disrespect.

         God wants order and respect in the family. He does not want you to hit your parents or to curse them either. Do you know young people who say bad things about their parents? That would have been worthy of death in the Old Testament. God is serious about the responsibility of family members to each other. We must teach young people about the responsibility they have toward their parents.

      (2) Proverbs 30:11-17

         (a) The problem

            You may identify with the description of unruly children in Proverbs 30. Much of it applies to young people today. Verse 11 says, "There is a generation that curseth their father, and doth not bless their mother." In many cases, mothers and fathers don't deserve honor, but that doesn't exempt the children from honoring them.

Verse 12 says, "There is a generation that are pure in their own eyes, and yet are not washed from their filthiness." They think they have no need for their parents' instruction and assume they have all the answers. But they don't realize how bad off they are. Verses 13-14 say, "There is a generation, oh, how lofty are their eyes! And their eyelids are lifted up [in pride]. There is a generation, whose teeth are like swords, and their jaw teeth like knives, to devour the poor from off the earth, and the needy from among men." When a prideful younger generation grows up, it takes advantage of others. We have seen evidence of that in America. Some of the nation's finest men compromised their principles for personal gain in incidents such as Watergate.

(b) The picture

Verse 15 illustrates prideful rebellion: "The horseleach hath two daughters, crying, Give, give." A horseleach is an insect that leaches blood from horses. A prideful generation is like a horseleach in that it takes anything it can out of society yet is never satisfied.

(c) The punishment

Verse 17 says, "The eye that mocketh at his father, and despiseth to obey his mother, the ravens of the valley shall pick it out, and the young eagles shall eat it." That's strong language. When you read something like that, you get the idea that God is serious about children honoring their parents.

The Pastor Who Cared for His Kids

One of the great disasters in the ministry occurs when pastors don't take care of their families because they are too busy with other things. I remember hearing Dr. Howard Hendricks of Dallas Theological Seminary relate a personal incident. Someone called him and said, "Dr. Hendricks, we're having a Bible conference, and we want you to be our speaker. Can you come?" Hendricks politely declined. The conference planner replied, "This is a crucial event for our whole community. Why can't you come? Do you have another appointment?" Hendricks said, "No. I've got to play with my kids." "You've got to play with your kids?" questioned the planner. "Don't you realize that our people need your instruction?" "Yes. But my kids also need me." Dr. Hendricks was right. If a man of his far-reaching influence ever lost the respect of his kids, the credibility of his ministry would be gone.

b) Illustrated

It's not wrong to play with your kids, especially if you want to avoid ending up like Eli, the Old Testament priest. He took care of everyone else's spiritual problems but apparently never took care of his own children. His sons, Hophni and Phinehas, turned out to be wicked men. In effect, God told Eli, "When I initiated the priesthood, I told Aaron and the others that they would be priests forever through the Aaronic lineage. But your sons have violated My law to such an extent that I'm going to halt the priestly ministry of your family. To validate these words, Hophni and Phinehas are going to die the same day" (cf. 1 Sam. 2:27-34). Eli's heart was broken after hearing that.

I'll never forget a story I heard from a man who was constantly involved in evangelistic meetings. He overheard his boy asking a neighbor to play. The other boy said, "I can't do anything with you because I've got to go with my dad. We're going to the park to play." The evangelist's son said, "Oh, my dad can't play with me; he's too busy playing with other people's children." The evangelist said few things ever affected him as much as that did.

Christians have an obligation to their families. A strong Christian family should be a high priority. And there is a high price to pay if we don't make that a priority. Therefore, we must strive to develop solid marriages and family-oriented ministries by teaching husbands to love their wives (Eph. 5:25), wives to submit to their husbands (5:22), children to obey their parents (6:1), and parents not to exasperate their children but nurture them (6:4).

VIII. BIBLE TEACHING AND PREACHING

A. The Focal Point

At the heart of a dynamic church is solid teaching and preaching. You can't make up for that with an anemic pulpit that offers sermonettes for Christianettes or with pious platitudes and entertaining stories. The heartbeat of the church is a dynamic presentation of the truth of God.

The Blessing of Verse-by-Verse Preaching

When W. A. Criswell went to the First Baptist Church of Dallas, he was only the second pastor in its history. (He succeeded another great man of God, George Truett.) When Criswell took over the pulpit, he told the board that he planned to teach the Bible verse by verse. Perhaps some were concerned that no one would come, but the church went on to be one of the largest in the world, with nearly 18,000 members. (His eventful life's story is told in *W. A. Criswell*, by Billy Keith [Old Tappan, N.J.: Revell], 1973.) People came because he taught them the Word of God. Their lives changed as they understood and responded to it.

There is no substitute for Bible teaching from the pulpit. That is the church's rallying point—the one common denominator that propels the church forward. Without it church members could not effectively grow in their spiritual lives.

B. The False Priorities

1. No preaching

Some have suggested that we shouldn't have churches like those we have today—that we should get rid of the buildings and make the family the common unit of Christian assembly, with the father serving as the priest. That setup would be ideal in theory, except that many fathers don't practice that ideal. And if they won't teach their wives and kids, someone else has to. Such a program might work to some extent, but ultimately it would fail because of the absence of a definite preaching ministry.

If you examine the life of Christ and the book of Acts, you will find that preaching was a constantly recurring theme. You can't eliminate what God uses because everyone doesn't accept it. First Corinthians 1:18 says, "The preaching of the cross is to them that perish foolishness; but unto us who are saved it is the power of God."

The proclamation of God's truth by preaching (Gk., *kērugma*) and teaching (Gk., *didachē*) changes lives. That is why all dynamic churches teach biblical truth and motivate Christians to apply it.

2. Positive preaching

Some believe that preaching should make everyone feel good. Suppose a man has an unhappy life: he works hard for an unfair boss, he's henpecked at home, his kid is a delinquent, and he can't make the payments on his car. When he comes to church, he shouldn't be smashed from pillar to post. Therefore some think that preaching ought to emphasize positive thinking that assumes that everything is wonderful and rosy.

I once saw a Christian television program where the preacher said, "Oh, every day with Jesus is so happy! If you could only be as happy as I am!" However, that wouldn't go over very well with a wife who has just returned from the cemetery where she buried her husband, or with a mother whose little child has been diagnosed with terminal leukemia. Every day is not a happy day. Every day is fulfilling, and there is an abiding joy in the presence of Christ, but Christianity is not a slap-happy way of life. If all we do is come together and tell each other how wonderful life is, then we're lying.

3. Problem preaching

Others think preaching should be geared toward helping people solve their problems. We live in a world that is so psychology oriented that it seems as if some people can barely think without getting into clinical analysis. We can no longer objectively accept anything without analyzing it. That reasoning has carried over into the church and has produced what I call "problem-centered preaching." That is where the preacher states a problem and takes ten verses out of context to show how to solve it, along with a few stories about some people who solved it.

A pastor is not a glorified psychoanalyst, a grandfather, or a Santa Claus who pats you on the head and tells you everything is fine. His task is to educate Christians in the Word of God and encourage them to change their behavior in accordance with it. In many cases it is better for a person to feel worse before he feels better because there has to be healing before there can be restoration. When I preach a sermon that convicts those who hear it, I know the message is getting through. A church pulpit isn't primarily designed to help people make decisions about the details of everyday living. It is meant to teach them the Word of God and identify sin so that they might change their behavior. Explaining one's problems doesn't make a person feel better. Rather, confession, repentance, and changing one's life are what produce true joy and enable the individual to deal with one's problems.

IX. A WILLINGNESS TO CHANGE

There's nothing sacred about tradition. We must distinguish carefully between what is unchangeable and what must be changed. A dynamic church should regularly burst out of old methods that are no longer effective. Note also that faith demands risk. A church can become so comfortable with unchanging forms that its members lose sight of what they are there for. But if a church lives on the precipice of change, there will be a sense of vitality.

A. The Issues of Change vs. Tradition

1. The times of worship

The church hasn't always had the same format for the worship service that we have today. The apostle Paul adapted to change. He taught anywhere between one and seven days a week. That intensity in preaching takes place today in some places in Africa, where many Christians gather at daybreak on Sunday and return home when the sun goes down.

I've preached in black churches in the South where I would finish one sermon and the congregation would say, "Brother, preach another one!" I'd turn the page in my notebook and take off on another passage. I have preached as many as three or four sermons in a row in situations like that. Contrast that with the more prevalent attitude of twelve o'clockitis: "It's twelve o'clock, and the sermon is still going! Give me a break!"

Some people aren't adaptable to change. They would collapse if there were no Sunday morning worship. Suppose we said, "We won't be meeting on Sunday mornings anymore because of the energy crisis. Therefore, we're going to meet in different places around the city on Tuesday evening." That shouldn't be a major problem for any believer because every day is sacred to the Christian. We enjoy being together on the day of the week that commemorates our Lord's resurrection, but that shouldn't prevent us from changing when it is necessary to do so.

2. The place of worship

Many people wrongly identify the church as the building itself. Christendom has canonized the form of the church and then has struggled to make it relevant. We live with incidental patterns for the church that we have made into institutions.

Many Christians retreat from the world to the church because they feel secure there. That thinking illustrates how threatened some Christians feel. That they find security in a building is a sign that they want to identify with something, and that's not bad in itself. People like routine because it's much less threatening than constant change. But bricks aren't sacred, and the order of worship is not inspired. There must be change in a church, or it will stagnate. True fellowship results from the presence of God's Spirit. God is busy not just on Sunday mornings but throughout the week in the lives of His people. He doesn't work in buildings; He works in the hearts of people.

How to Be Flexible

There are three keys to help a church maintain flexibility.

1. Recognize that spiritual life takes precedence over structure

What goes on in a Christian's life outside the church is more important than what goes on within its walls. The church building is not God's house; the believer is (1 Cor. 6:19). Greek scholar Kenneth Wuest translates 2 Corinthians 6:16 as follows: "As for us, we are an inner sanctuary of the living God" (*The New Testament, An Expanded Translation* [Grand Rapids: Eerdmans, 1980], p. 426).

2. Be open to the Holy Spirit

If the Holy Spirit is the One behind change, believers should be ready and willing to change.

3. Make sure that procedure follows needs

To remain spiritually alive, a church must adapt to the needs of the people. If society changes, then the church must be flexible so that it can minister effectively. A church must not say, "We've never done it that way before," if that's the way God wants it done now.

B. The Illustration of Change vs. Tradition

Some people easily confuse a form, which is changeable, with truth, which is unchangeable. They often assume that the church—the bastion of truth—is an unchangeable form.

1. The context

Matthew 15:1 says, "Then came to Jesus scribes and Pharisees, who were of Jerusalem." The scribes and Pharisees continually found fault with what Jesus and His disciples were doing. The scribes had instituted a plethora of rules that were not binding in God's eyes. Those rabbinical traditions were not laws inspired by God. Rather, they were legalistic rules that enabled people to exalt themselves since they could keep them more easily than the true laws of God.

2. The confusion

One of the rules the scribes established was that before they ate, they had to go through a ceremonial procedure of purifying themselves. It was a meaningless religious exercise. Jesus' disciples didn't follow those procedures. Therefore, the Pharisees and scribes accused them of breaking tradition, saying in verse 2, "Why do thy disciples transgress the tradition of the elders? For they wash not their hands when they eat bread."

When our church changed the order of the worship service and put some music at the end, someone asked why we did that. He liked the music at the beginning of the service because we'd always had it at the beginning. He was bound by a tradition with relatively little significance. He needed to understand that human tradition can never be equated with divine authorization.

3. The contrast

Jesus answered the legalists who sought to condemn Him, saying, "Why do ye also transgress the commandment of God by your tradition?" (v. 3). That the disciples didn't obey rabbinic traditions was of little consequence compared to the scribes and Pharisees' disobedience to God's commands. Jesus elaborated on His justified condemnation of them by saying, "For God commanded, saying, Honor thy father and mother; and, He that curseth father or mother, let him die the death" (v. 4). That commandment required a child to respect and care for his parents. But instead of providing financially for their parents, the scribes and Pharisees justified their disobedience by "consecrating" their money to God (vv. 5-6). Jesus called them hypocrites for accusing His disciples of breaking their arbitrary traditions while they were disobeying God's authoritative laws (v. 7).

4. The condemnation

Jesus then quoted Isaiah's prophetic indictment of the Jewish leaders: "In vain they do worship me, teaching for doctrines the commandments of men" (v. 9; Isa. 29:13). They didn't know the difference between what was tradition and what was divine command. In a similar way, the church has confused people so that they don't know the difference between what God instituted and what the church instituted.

X. GREAT FAITH

Great churches live on the precipice of faith where they can do nothing but trust God. They are accustomed to the tension of trusting God and accepting the risk that is inseparable from faith.

A. Exemplified

Consider Moses and how he stretched the faith of the Israelites. He led them out of Egypt, assuring them that God would protect them. When they reached the Red Sea, Pharaoh's army caught up to them. But just in time God parted the Red Sea. Then trusting in the Lord, the people passed safely to the other side whereas Pharaoh's army was drowned. Once they were on the other side, the people wanted to know what they were going to do. So Moses explained that they were going to go through the desert to the Promised Land. Then the people wanted to know what they were to do for food. Moses said that God would drop food out of heaven for them.

B. Exhorted

One cannot live a godly life without risk. Because faith is inseparable from risk, it is ironic that Christians generally dislike anything risky. Ephesians 3:20 says God "is able to do exceedingly abundantly above all that we ask or think, according to the power that works within us," and we need to believe Him for that. Hebrews 11 lists heroes of faith who believed God and took risks. That's another way of saying they trusted in Him. Daniel believed God in a lions' den. Abraham believed God when Sarah was too old to have a baby, and God sent the promised child.

Christianity's approach is not "a bird in the hand is worth two in the bush." Christians should not be afraid of moving ahead with new ideas. Unfortunately, that's what happens in many churches. People who want to move out for God are often restrained by those who hold the purse strings and lack great faith. The latter create a bottleneck that prevents God's work from expanding. A church may have all kinds of great plans, but if the people can't trust God to supply the manpower and the money, those plans will never be accomplished. God does not have a problem getting money for what He wants done. Faith work wonders, and it is exciting to see that.

XI. SACRIFICE

A spirit of sacrifice is directly related to the previous point. The leadership of an effective church doesn't have to plead for its people to be involved or to give because the congregation's faith should enable them to stretch themselves sacrificially. It shouldn't have a need for gimmicks, drives, and artificial means of stimulating its people to do what they ought to do. The members of such a church have a sacrificial spirit of giving such as the Macedonians had, who poured out love by giving "beyond their ability" (2 Cor. 8:3, NASB). Paul commended the Philippians for meeting his needs (Phil. 4:10, 14-16). He didn't have to ask them for anything because their love abounded to him generously and tangibly.

XII. WORSHIPING GOD

What especially makes a church great is its emphasis on worship. A church can emphasize many things that are good. But often those things are overemphasized, and the means become the end. When a program becomes an end in itself, anything becomes permissible in the process of accomplishing it. In such cases there is no base of integrity, and the church compromises its principles.

Some churches' entire orientation is around their theological distinctives. They claim to be the only ones who believe a certain way. Sometimes those distinctives are part of their title. They might be the First Sovereign, Premillennial, Pretribulational, Anti-liberal, Proconservative, Uncompromising Church of Oak Street. Strong biblical theology is important, but the thrust of the church is more than that.

Churches that glorify their uniqueness often become caricatures. Some churches focus entirely on the Person of Christ. I'm not against focusing on Christ, but I'm concerned about churches that act as if the rest of the Trinity doesn't exist. In a similar way, other churches focus primarily on the Holy Spirit. In contrast to those imbalanced approaches, the church is to be preoccupied with the entire Trinity. The church is to worship God in His fullness.

When a church sets its complete focus on God and does everything it can to honor Him, it has a base for uncompromising integrity. It doesn't matter what makes the church unique or what theological distinctive it has. What matters is God's requirements.

Conclusion

May the twelve marks of an effective church be the basis of every Christian church so that God may be fully honored.

Focusing on the Facts

1. Why can't church members merely walk in and out of church and say they are involved (see p. 25)?
2. According to Hebrews 10:24-25, why do we go to church (see pp. 25-26)?
3. What are some of the responses we are to have toward other believers (see p. 26)?
4. Give some examples of how Jesus showed His intense concern for others (see pp. 26-28).
5. What has the trend toward the family been in the modern church (see p. 28)?
6. What were the consequences in the Old Testament for striking or cursing one's parents? What does that tell us about God's perspective on respecting authority (see p. 29)?
7. What mistake did Eli the priest make in handling his ministry and his sons (see p. 31)?
8. What are some keys to having a healthy family according to Ephesians 5-6 (see p. 32)?
9. What should be the focal point of a dynamic church's ministry (see p. 32)?
10. Should every day be a happy day for a Christian? Explain (see pp. 33-34).
11. What is a preacher's task with regard to his congregation and the Word of God (see p. 34)?
12. What should be a church's attitude toward change (see p. 35)?
13. In what way do many people wrongly identify the church (see p. 36)?
14. How can a church maintain an attitude of flexibility (see pp. 36-37)?

15. Explain how the scribes and Pharisees confused changeable form with unchangeable truth (Matt. 15:1-9; see pp. 37-38).
16. Explain the relation of faith to risk (see pp. 38-39).
17. Why doesn't the leadership of an effective church have to plead for its people to be involved or to provide financial support (see p. 40)?
18. What group of Christians did Paul commend for their sacrificial spirit of giving (see p. 40)?
19. What should the church's primary goal be? What can happen when a church overemphasizes its programs (see p. 40)?

Pondering the Principles

1. Are you instructing your children to respect you as parents? Do they see a respect for authority in your own life? Do you honor your parents, obey governmental laws, and treat your employer with respect? Or do your children see indifference as you justify bending society's rules and regulations? Do they see hypocrisy in your life and therefore lose respect for you? Or do they see uncompromising integrity in your life and honor you by following your example? Do you spend time with your children so that you can teach them your godly value system? If your family is struggling to be the kind of loving family God desires, make sure you invest time in serving and communicating with each other. Consult the numerous books and tape series available on the subject of the family. If your church is lacking a ministry to families, prayerfully consider with your pastor how that need might be met.

2. Faith demands risk. You may be trusting God to work through your life, but are you risking anything? Are you taking chances with your comfort, future plans, popularity, job, or life as you serve the Lord in faith? Are you willing to risk those things to live a life of dependency on Him? Read Hebrews 11. What risks did the Old Testament characters take, knowing that God is faithful in His promises? In spite of the temporary hazards you may encounter, begin trusting God for things that will stretch your faith. Then when He does them, you will know to give Him the credit.

3
What in the World Is the Church to Be?—Part 1

Outline

Introduction
A. The Invisible Church
B. The Visible Church

Lesson
I. The Founding of the Church
   A. Its Members
   B. Its Beginning
   C. Its Makeup
   D. Its Leadership
      1. Spiritual delegation
      2. Spirit-led direction
II. The Ministry of the Church
   A. The Pattern Established
   B. The Practice Exhorted
III. The Leadership of the Church
   A. The Categories of Leadership
      1. Elders
         a) Their responsibilities
            (1) Making godly decisions
            (2) Defending the Word
            (3) Disciplining wayward members
         b) Their qualifications
            (1) As listed in 1 Timothy 3

43

Introduction

The description of the early church in Acts 2:42-47 gives us a basic outline of what God intends the church of Jesus Christ to be: "[It] continued steadfastly in the apostles' doctrine and fellowship, and in breaking of bread, and in prayers. And fear came upon every soul; and many wonders and signs were done by the apostles. And all that believed were together, and had all things common; and sold their possessions and goods, and parted them to all men, as every man had need. And they, continuing daily with one accord in the temple, and breaking bread from house to house, did eat their food with gladness and singleness of heart, praising God, and having favor with all the people. And the Lord added to the church daily such as should be saved."

A. The Invisible Church

We who love Jesus Christ constitute the true church. We belong to the collective Body of Christ whether we're alive or in glory. The Greek word for church is *ekklēsia*, which means "an assembly of called-out ones." The church is made up of people called by God to be His children. We have become united with all other believers by faith in Christ, who said, "I will build my church, and the gates of [hades] shall not prevail against it" (Matt. 16:18). Jesus meant He would gather together a body of believers. He wasn't talking about buildings; He was talking about people. We who know and love Him are the living church that has been born into the family of God by the Holy Spirit. As members of "the general assembly and church of the first-born, who are written in heaven" (Heb. 12:23), we have been declared righteous because our sin has been washed away by the blood of Jesus Christ (Rev. 1:5).

B. The Visible Church

The world cannot detect the invisible church of real Christians. They see only the visible church of those who profess to be Christians. The Lord intended the visible church to be a testimony to the world. When we gather together on the Lord's Day, we are a testimony to the world that Christ has indeed risen.

Some say we don't need buildings or organizational structure. However, I don't think Christ would have agreed. In Matthew 18 He implies that the church would meet together in a given place: "If thy brother shall trespass against thee, go and tell him his fault between thee and him alone; if he shall hear thee, thou hast gained thy brother. But if he will not hear thee, then take with thee one or two more, that in the mouth of two or three witnesses every word may be established. And if he shall neglect to hear them, *tell it unto the church*" (vv. 15-17, emphasis added). He must have been referring to a visible group of people, even though the church did not officially exist until Pentecost (Acts 2:1-4). In the context of Matthew 18, we see the church as a visible assembly of believers engaged in the discipline process.

In the book of Acts we see the invisible church becoming more visible. Although the visible and invisible church were initially the same, the picture changed as false believers associated with the church. Today there are visible congregations meeting that are not the true church at all. Rather, they are part of the false church, which is called "the great harlot" (Rev. 17:1). The invisible church became visible as believers began to gather together. Originally they met in homes, but by the third century the church was meeting in its own building as it continued to grow.

Let's examine three biblical aspects of the church: the founding of the church, the ministry of the church, and the leadership of the church. Although there are new ways to communicate, new methods to use, and new problems to deal with in the twentieth century, I believe the Lord intends the church of this century to follow the same basic principles as the first-century church.

Lesson

I. THE FOUNDING OF THE CHURCH

A. Its Members

The first local assembly met in Jerusalem. It consisted primarily of humble people: fishermen, farmers, and other poor people. But some were well off since they had goods they were willing to share with the tremendous number of needy people in the church (Acts 2:44-45). Furthermore, since Christians were ostracized for their faith in Christ, it was also necessary for them to share among themselves.

Incidentally, having all things in common was not the practice of any other church mentioned in the book of Acts. It was practiced in Jerusalem only because of the tremendous number of poor believers and the unusual circumstances of the church there.

B. Its Beginning

The church at Jerusalem was born in a prayer meeting on the Day of Pentecost. The Spirit came and filled those who were waiting in an upper room. As a result, they experienced a dramatic manifestation of the unity of the Spirit and the love of Christ, which caused the church to grow rapidly. In fact, it acquired three thousand new Christians on the first day (Acts 2:41).

How did that happen so fast? The ministry of the Holy Spirit uniquely brought it all to pass. When the three thousand were saved—many of whom were visiting from other places—they returned to their homes, and even more were added to the rapidly growing church. That was one way the church spread throughout the land of Israel.

C. Its Makeup

Acts 2:42 gives the basic ingredients of church life: "They continued steadfastly in the apostles' doctrine and fellowship, and in breaking of bread [communion], and in prayers." The only other thing you can add to that was the preaching of the good news of Jesus Christ. They proclaimed it in the streets, in the Temple, in homes, and everywhere they could. As a result, "the Lord added to the church daily such as should be saved" (v. 47). They had all the ingredients necessary for a God-blessed, Spirit-directed church. There were no gimmicks. The Holy Spirit directed the ministry, and the people followed His leading.

Today churches often use gimmicks and entertainment to try to get people into church. Such ploys indicate that the people in those churches aren't following the biblical pattern or depending on the Spirit's leading.

The church at Jerusalem had a social life—it wasn't all business and no fellowship. They had the love-feast, which was the early church's version of a pot-luck dinner. Unfortunately, the church at Corinth had problems with that practice: the rich were eating their own pot-luck dishes and were allowing the poor to go hungry. The ministry of sharing food and fellowship at the love-feast deteriorated into selfishness—a problem Paul had to correct (1 Cor. 11:17-34). Nevertheless in the beginning, the church met together for fellowship around the table and ate together, sharing their food. People freely ministered to each other.

Did the Early Church Live in Communes?

The church was never designed to be a commune; that is not a New Testament concept. In Acts 5 Ananias and Sapphira sell a piece of property and promise to give the proceeds to the Lord (vv. 1-2). However, they lied about the amount they sold it for and gave only a portion to the church, claiming it was the full price (v. 2). When Peter confronted their sin he said, "While it remained, was it not thine own?" (v. 4). That statement reveals that there was no injunction for believers to sell their property and turn it over to the church. Peter did not expect them or other believers to turn over all their assets to the church. The problem was that they "lied [not] unto men, but unto God" (v. 4). The problem was not that they sold their property and kept some of the money from God. The problem was that they claimed they would give Him a certain amount but didn't. They tried to give a false impression to the church without any regard for God. Since the church was newly founded and discipline had to be strict, they were both killed instantly for lying to the Holy Spirit.

D. Its Leadership

1. Spiritual delegation

The twelve apostles led the early church until elders and deacons were trained to lead and serve in other congregations. The apostles were with the Jerusalem church for at least seven years and did all the work, including the serving of food, until they chose seven men to relieve them of that responsibility (Acts 6:1-6). Some of these men had developed to the place of spiritual leadership and maturity so that they became evangelists and teaching pastors (vv. 7-8).

2. Spirit-led direction

After several years, the apostles were ready to send out other leaders to establish and minister to new churches. In fact, they nurtured the Jerusalem church for seven years before they sent people out to minister elsewhere. I would imagine that since Christianity started at a such a small place, the apostles would have been anxious to see it spread around the world. Yet in the Spirit's wisdom, they waited for His direction to begin an official missionary outreach.

Paul, Silas, Barnabas, and others planted several independent churches. Since each church was ultimately led by the Holy Spirit, they were all one in the Spirit. The early Christians had a common bond. In Romans 16:16 Paul says, "The churches of Christ greet you." There was a oneness among the independent congregations. They were composed of Jews and Gentiles and all classes of believers: rich, poor, educated, and uneducated. Christians from a wide spectrum of society were functioning together as one. The only organizational structure they had was that which was instituted by the Holy Spirit.

The church has changed a great deal over the centuries. It has become very complex and businesslike. Today it is a massive organization with denominations, commissions, committees, councils, boards, and programs. It quite often functions like a business rather than a body, a factory rather than a family, a corporation rather than a community.

The church today has also become obsessed with success, establishing superficial goals and awarding prizes to those who can pack the most people into the pews on Sundays, although the teaching is insipid or there are spiritual problems. Many church leaders panic when the line starts dropping on the graph, indicating a drop in attendance and finances.

Churches have become entertainment centers, giving performances to placid, unproductive churchgoers. Most of the devices are geared to get people into church but do not do anything with them once they come.

II. THE MINISTRY OF THE CHURCH

I want to look at three New Testament epistles—1 and 2 Timothy and Titus—because they tell us what the ministry and organizational structure of the church should be. Timothy and Titus were evangelists. In the early church, an evangelist was a church planter who went to an area where there were no Christians, won people to Christ, and established a congregation. Usually he would remain with that congregation as long as a year and maybe even longer, until he had taught them sufficiently. When some of them had matured, he would then appoint elders in that city to care for the church and teach it. Then he would move to another place and do the same thing all over again.

The letters to Timothy and Titus establish the pattern for the church's behavior. For example, Paul wrote to Timothy saying, "These things write I unto thee, hoping to come unto thee shortly; but if I tarry long, that thou mayest know how thou oughtest to behave thyself in the house of God, which is the church of the living God, the pillar and ground of the truth" (1 Tim. 3:14-15).

A. The Pattern Established

The basic task of the church is to teach sound doctrine. It is not to give some pastor's opinion, recite tear-jerking illustrations, raise funds, present programs and entertainment, or give weekly devotionals.

1. Titus 2:1—"Speak thou the things which become sound doctrine." Evangelists such as Titus moved into an area and taught sound doctrine to newly established churches.

2. 1 Timothy 1:3, 6-7, 10—Paul said to Timothy, "Charge some that they teach no other doctrine" (v. 3). When a church doesn't have a constant diet of sound doctrine, some people turn "aside unto vain jangling" (v. 6)— they follow every new idea that comes along. They desire "to be teachers of the law, understanding neither what they say, nor that about which they affirm" (v. 7). If sound doctrine isn't taught, the people will gravitate toward teaching that is not sound.

The Greek word translated "sound doctrine" in verse 10 means "healthy" (we get the English word *hygienic* from it). Sound doctrine from the Word of God builds the Body of Christ. Any other kind of doctrine tears it apart and has no place in the church.

How to Protect a Church Against False Doctrine

First Timothy 4:1-2 says, "The Spirit speaketh expressly that, in the latter times, some shall depart from the faith, giving heed to seducing spirits, and doctrines of demons, speaking lies in hypocrisy, having their conscience seared with a hot iron." How can the church be protected from seducing spirits and doctrines of demons?

1. The protection of preaching

Verses 6-7 say, "If thou put the brethren in remembrance of these things, thou shalt be a good minister of Jesus Christ, nourished up in the words of faith and of good doctrine, unto which thou hast attained. But refuse profane and old wives' fables, and exercise thyself rather unto godliness." The only way a church can protect itself from false doctrine is by nourishing the people in sound doctrine.

2. The pattern of preaching

Verse 13 says, "Give attendance to reading, to exhortation, to doctrine." Those three elements form the essence of preaching: reading Scripture, declaring it, and explaining it. That's what expository preaching is all about. An expository preacher must read and explain the text, then exhort his congregation to follow the principles contained in it, telling them how. The Greek word translated "reading" refers to the public reading of Scripture associated with a preaching ministry.

3. The preparation for preaching

Verse 15 says, "Meditate upon these things; give thyself wholly to them." The leadership of the church is to be engaged in a concentrated study of the Word of God, not in anything else. Rather than be distracted by a multitude of extraneous activities, the leaders are to be absorbed in doctrine.

4. The priority of preaching

Verse 16 says, "Take heed unto thyself and unto the doctrine; continue in them; for in doing this thou shalt both save thyself and them that hear thee." Demonic teachers who attempt to infiltrate the church will be cast aside when the church is faithfully involved in teaching sound doctrine. Pastors are to give themselves fully to teaching the truth.

If the church of Jesus Christ is to be protected from false doctrine, the elders who lead it must be faithful to teach sound doctrine. As a minister of Jesus Christ, I am first of all responsible to God for the purity of the church and its protection from false doctrine. All ministers of the gospel are answerable to Christ for how faithfully they protect and nurture the flock. Unfortunately, there are many pastors whose churches expect them to do everything but what Christ intends—teach the Word of God. Their energies are dissipated into other duties rather than their prime duty.

B. The Practice Exhorted

1. 2 Timothy 1:13-14—"Hold fast the form of sound words, which thou hast heard of me, in faith and love which is

in Christ Jesus. That good thing which was committed unto thee keep by the Holy Spirit, who dwelleth in us." The Greek word translated "form" implies that the regular practice of instruction for the church should be teaching sound words.

2. 2 Timothy 2:1-2—"Thou, therefore, my son, be strong in the grace that is in Christ Jesus. And the things that thou hast heard from me among many witnesses, the same commit thou to faithful men, who shall be able to teach others also." A pastor teaches his congregation sound doctrine so that they can teach it to others. The elders are to help the saints mature so that they can do the work of the ministry (Eph. 4:11-12).

3. 2 Timothy 2:15—"Study to show thyself approved unto God, a workman that needeth not to be ashamed, rightly dividing the word of truth." The effective ministry is centered on teaching doctrine, and the key is diligent study.

4. 2 Timothy 2:24-25—"The servant of the Lord must not strive, but be gentle unto all men, apt to teach, patient, in meekness instructing those that oppose him, if God, perhaps, will give them repentance to the acknowledging of the truth." When correcting people, do not have a belligerent attitude; rather show love and meekness.

5. 2 Timothy 3:14-17—"Continue thou in the things which thou hast learned and hast been assured of, knowing of whom thou hast learned them, and that from a child thou hast known the holy scriptures, which are able to make thee wise unto salvation through faith which is in Christ Jesus. All scripture is given by inspiration of God, and is profitable for doctrine, for reproof, for correction, for instruction in righteousness, that the man of God may be perfect, thoroughly furnished unto all good works." If Christians are to become spiritually mature, then church leaders must preach from all of Scripture.

6. 2 Timothy 4:1-2—"I charge thee, therefore, before God, and the Lord Jesus Christ, who shall judge the living and the dead at his appearing and his kingdom: preach

the word; be diligent in season, out of season; reprove, rebuke, exhort with all long-suffering and doctrine."

The ministry of the church is simple: to preach sound doctrine in the pattern of the early evangelists.

III. THE LEADERSHIP OF THE CHURCH

A. The Categories of Leadership

There are two categories of leaders in the church: elders and deacons.

1. Elders

a) Their responsibilities

In the New Testament church, the leadership belonged collectively to a group of elders who were leaders under the Spirit of God. One man was not responsible for doing everything. The pastor is not the professional problem solver who runs around with an ecclesiastical bag of tools, waiting for the next problem to solve or the next squeaky wheel to grease.

An elder is also referred to as a "bishop" in the New Testament. *Elder* emphasizes his title, and *bishop*, meaning "overseer," refers to his duty. He oversees the flock. His is a spiritual ministry concerned with two things: prayer and teaching God's Word.

(1) Making godly decisions

The elders who rule in the local church are first responsible to Christ—not to the congregation or a council. First Timothy 5:17 says, "Let the elders that rule well be counted worthy of double honor, especially they who labor in the word and doctrine." Not all are necessarily involved in teaching doctrine; there are other capacities in the design of the Spirit.

All elders, however, are responsible for making decisions after prayer and Bible study so that they can be made unanimously with the mind of Christ (1 Cor. 2:16) in the energy of the Spirit. Only then can they lead the church with positive effects for the entire congregation. Ruling as an elder is a high calling.

(2) Defending the Word

Titus 1:9-11 says an elder should be "holding fast the faithful word as he hath been taught, that he may be able by sound doctrine both to exhort and to confute the opposers. For there are many unruly and vain talkers and deceivers, specially they of the circumcision, whose mouths must be stopped, who subvert whole houses, teaching things which they ought not, for filthy lucre's sake." The elders are to keep false teachers out.

(3) Disciplining wayward members

Elders are to discipline Christians who fall into doctrinal error. Second Timothy 2:17-18 speaks of the destructive teaching of "Hymenaeus and Philetus, who, concerning the truth, have erred, saying that the resurrection is past already; and overthrow the faith of some." Paul recognized that as a serious problem that had to be dealt with.

First Timothy 1:20 records how he dealt with Hymenaeus and Alexander: "I have delivered [them] unto Satan, that they may learn not to blaspheme." When a person teaches doctrinal error, he is to be put out of the fellowship until Satan has brought him to the place where he is willing to abandon his error. Then God can begin to restore him.

First Timothy 5:20 says, "Them that sin rebuke before all, that others also may fear." Elders have the right and the obligation to rebuke sin publicly.

b) Their qualifications

Elders were ordained in every city where there was a church (Titus 1:5). They were chosen out of the congregation. A church is strongest, I'm convinced, when its own people are a part of its leadership.

(1) As listed in 1 Timothy 3

First Timothy 3 lists what is required of an elder: "If a man desire the office of a bishop, he desireth a good work. A bishop then must be blameless [he must have a good reputation among believers], the husband of one wife [faithful to his one and only wife], temperate, sober-minded, of good behavior, given to hospitality, apt to teach [able to communicate his faith]; not given [addicted] to wine, not violent, not greedy of filthy lucre [money], but patient, not a brawler, not covetous; one that ruleth well his own house, having his children in subjection with all gravity [seriousness] (for if a man know not how to rule his own house, how shall he take care of the church of God?); not a novice [recent convert], lest being lifted up with pride he fall into the condemnation of the devil. Moreover, he must have a good report of them who are outside, lest he fall into reproach and the snare of the devil" (vv. 1-7).

The highest position of authority in the church belongs to elders, who rule under Christ, the Great Shepherd, as His undershepherds (1 Pet. 5:2-4). They are responsible for teaching doctrine, administrating, disciplining, protecting the flock, praying for the flock, and studying the Word of God. They are answerable to Jesus Christ for their ministry.

Focusing on the Facts

1. In what sense is the true church invisible? Who constitutes the church of Jesus Christ (see p. 44)?

2. Why did the Lord intend for there to be a visible church? How does Matthew 18 support that (see pp. 44-45)?

3. Although the invisible and visible churches were initially the same, what caused them to become different (see p. 45)?

4. What type of people did the Jerusalem church primarily consist of? Why was it necessary for that church to share their possessions? Was that degree of sharing a common practice in other churches mentioned in the book of Acts (see pp. 45-46)?

5. Explain how the church at Jerusalem was born. How was it able to spread throughout the land of Israel at such an early stage (see p. 46)?

6. What were the four basic ingredients of church life according to Acts 2:42? What else could be added to that (see p. 46)?

7. Why do some churches resort to using gimmicks and entertainment? What does that indicate (see p. 47)?

8. Explain how Acts 5 verifies that the Jerusalem church did not practice communal living where the members forfeited their own possessions (see p. 47).

9. Who were the first leaders of the early church? As the church spread, who were chosen and trained to lead and serve in other congregations (see p. 48)?

10. Did the Jerusalem church immediately send out leaders to establish and strengthen other churches? Explain (see p. 48).

11. How has the church changed over the centuries (see pp. 48-49)?

12. Describe the function of an evangelist in the early church (see p. 49).

13. What is the basic task of the church? Support your answer with Scripture (see pp. 49-50).

14. What does sound doctrine do for the Body of Christ? What will any other kind of doctrine do (see p. 50)?

15. How can a church be protected against false doctrine (see pp. 50-51)?

16. What does Ephesians 4:11-12 say about the ministry of elders (see p. 52)?

17. What are the two offices of leadership in the church today? To which office does the word *bishop* refer (see p. 53)?

18. To whom are the elders that rule in the local church responsible (see p. 53)?

19. How should elders make decisions (see pp. 53-54)?

20. What is the ministry of elders regarding discipline (see p. 54)?

Pondering the Principles

1. Is the church you attend continuing "steadfastly in the apostles' doctrine and fellowship, and in breaking of bread, and in prayers" (Acts 2:42)? In which areas do you think it needs to be strengthened? How can you help to strengthen the weak areas? Can you pray, make suggestions, participate on a committee, or serve as an elder or deacon? How does your personal walk with the Lord rate in each of those four areas? Be sure to study Scripture on a regular basis and not just rely on the weekly sermon. Take advantage of fellowship opportunities with other Christians, make it a point to participate in the Lord's Table on a regular basis, and be sure to pray for your church and pastor. Be everything that you can be as an individual Christian, and your church will be sure to benefit.

2. Paul said to Timothy, "All Scripture is God-breathed and is useful for teaching, rebuking, correcting and training in righteousness, so that the man of God may be thoroughly equipped for every good work" (2 Tim. 3:16-17, NIV*). Are you letting Scripture thoroughly equip you by reading it, meditating on it, and studying it? Since God's plan is for us to live righteously, daily exercise your mind with God's Word so you can be trained in righteousness. Meditate on Joshua 1:8, Psalm 1:1-3, and James 1:21-25.

* *New International Version.*

4
What in the World Is the Church to Be?—Part 2

Outline

Introduction

Review
I. The Founding of the Church
II. The Ministry of the Church
III. The Leadership of the Church
  A. The Categories of Leadership
    1. Elders
      a) Their responsibilities
      b) Their qualifications
        (1) As listed in 1 Timothy 3

Lesson
        (2) As listed in Titus 1
      c) Their obligations
        (1) To examine themselves
        (2) To feed the church
    2. Deacons
      a) Their responsibilities
      b) Their qualifications
  B. The Congregation They Lead
    1. General duties
    2. Specific duties
      a) Of the men
        (1) To their family
        (2) To their employer
        (3) To each other
        (4) To God

    b) Of the women
        (1) To be modest
            (a) With godly fear
            (b) With sobriety
            (c) Without fancy apparel
            (d) With godly concerns
        (2) To learn in submission
        (3) To live righteously
        (4) To teach others

Introduction

All believers in Jesus Christ are a part of His church. Every Christian is positionally united in the Body of Christ by the Spirit of God. The church is a living community of people redeemed by Jesus Christ. However, individual Christians aren't always visible to the world because they obviously aren't marked by a tag identifying them as true believers. Satan commonly sows tares (false believers) among the wheat (true believers; Matt. 13:36-43). Therefore it is important to carefully evaluate a person's life before putting him in a position of Christian leadership.

Although spiritual life is essentially invisible and therefore difficult for the world to detect, God has designed the church to be visible to the world by its collective testimony to the power of the gospel. Tragically, it isn't as visible as it should be, and many who appear to be believers actually are not. Therefore the church often presents a confusing picture to the world, and that has been Satan's plan all along. The church's testimony must be clear for it to shine as a guiding light in the midst of the world's confusion.

Review

I. THE FOUNDING OF THE CHURCH (see pp. 45-49)

Acts 2:47 says that the Jerusalem church found "favor with all the people. And the Lord added to the church daily such as should be saved." The visible church in Jerusalem had a dynamic impact. It was a local assembly of believers who met together for study, fellowship, communion, and prayer. Then they went out spreading the gospel of Christ.

II. THE MINISTRY OF THE CHURCH (see pp. 49-53)

Many churches today don't fit the biblical pattern, having created inflexible traditions based on nonspecific biblical passages. They find themselves locked into a mold that is not adaptable to our day.

III. THE LEADERSHIP OF THE CHURCH

A. The Categories of Leadership

1. Elders

a) Their responsibilities (see pp. 53-54)

How Are Church Leaders to Be Chosen?

Acts 14:21-23 records the ordination of elders in the early church: "When [Paul and Barnabas] had preached the gospel to that city, and had taught many, they returned again to Lystra, and to Iconium, and Antioch, confirming the souls of the disciples, and exhorting them to continue in the faith, and that we must through much tribulation enter into the kingdom of God. And when they had ordained elders in every church, and had prayed with fasting, they commended them to the Lord, on whom they believed."

How does God indicate whom the leaders should be so that the church can ordain them? We can seek His wisdom through prayer and fasting, but in the end, the church is to base its decision on the qualifications clearly delineated in Scripture. Elders should not be chosen because of their knowledge of the business world, financial ability, prominence, or even their innate leadership abilities. They are to be chosen because God has obviously called and prepared them for the leadership of the church.

b) Their qualifications

(1) As listed in 1 Timothy 3 (see p. 55)

Lesson

(2) As listed in Titus 1

Besides writing to Timothy, Paul also wrote to Titus about the requirements for an elder: "For this cause left I thee in Crete, that thou shouldest set in order the things that are wanting, and ordain elders in every city, as I had appointed thee" (Titus 1:5). Note that in the New Testament the evangelist ordained the elders. Today there are very few church-planting evangelists. Today's evangelist is often much different from a biblical evangelist, who was responsible for ordaining elders who met certain spiritual qualifications.

In Titus 1:6 Paul says that men being considered as elders must be "blameless." That doesn't mean they have to be perfect. If that were true, we'd all be disqualified. It means there shouldn't be a great blot on a man's life that would provoke criticism by others.

Furthermore Paul said that an elder should be "the husband of one wife, having faithful children not accused of profligacy, or unruly" (v. 6). He must give evidence of having been effective in communicating his faith to his own family. Certainly you don't expect to see complete sainthood in the children, but they should be following their father's faith with a measure of godly conduct.

Verse 7 says that the bishop or elder "must be blameless, as the steward of God." He must realize he doesn't own anything but merely manages the affairs of God for the Body of Christ.

Also he must not be "self-willed, not soon angry, not given to wine." (v. 7). About the only thing people could drink in New Testament times was wine because pure water was difficult to obtain. The Greek term pictures one who stayed beside his wine a long time, giving evidence that he had a problem with alcohol.

Also an elder should not be "violent" or "given to filthy lucre" (v. 7). He doesn't react with his fists or pursue money as his primary goal.

On a positive note, verse 8 says that an elder should be "a lover of hospitality." He must be willing to open his home to strangers. And he will be able to because his household is well-managed (1 Tim. 3:4-5). An elder's home should display what Christian living is all about. Furthermore he is to be "a lover of good men, sober-minded, just, holy, temperate, holding fast the faithful word" (vv. 8-9). An elder should know his priorities and practice self-control as he lives by the standards of God's Word.

c) Their obligations

Acts 20 gives us a look at elders in Ephesus.

(1) To examine themselves

In verse 28 Paul says, "Take heed, therefore, unto yourselves, and to all the flock, over which the Holy Spirit hath made you overseers" (cf. 2 Cor. 13:5). An elder who rules the church must evaluate not only his own life but also the spiritual needs of his flock. We need to take note of everyone in the flock God has given us so that we can recognize and specifically pray for their individual problems and needs.

(2) To feed the church

Paul also exhorted the Ephesian elders "to feed the church of God" (v. 28). What is it that the church must feed on? The Word of God (1 Pet. 2:2; 1 Cor. 3:2). To be in control of doctrine and discipline in the church is a serious responsibility. Consequently it is an office of great honor and reward.

Peter said, "The elders who are among you I exhort, who am also an elder, and a witness of the sufferings of Christ, and also a partaker of the glory that shall be revealed: Feed the flock of God which is among you, taking the oversight of it" (1 Pet. 5:1-2). When a sheep was injured, the shepherd would care for it. Likewise, the spiritual shepherd needs to care for the flock of God.

Peter further said that overseeing the flock should not be done "by constraint [and] not for filthy lucre but of a ready mind" (v. 2). An elder should not serve as though his responsibility were a distasteful task but willingly because it is a privilege. His motivation shouldn't be to minister to rich people to receive a reward, but to minister eagerly to everyone.

Verse 3 says, "Neither as being lords over God's heritage, but being examples to the flock." The best way to lead is not by being a dictator but by being an example. If you try to lead people without setting a pattern that they can willingly follow, they will resist your leadership.

Leading by example has a wonderful reward: "When the chief Shepherd shall appear, ye shall receive a crown of glory that fadeth not away" (v. 4). And the worthy leaders who receive them will be able to cast them at the feet of Jesus Christ—the One to whom they really belong (Rev. 4:10).

2. Deacons

a) Their responsibilities

Acts 6 introduces us to a group whom many believe to be the first deacons. Although these men are never specifically called deacons, they are certainly appropriate models for deacons. Apparently it was sometime after this that the office of a deacon was officially recognized in the church.

In the earliest days of the church, the church at Jerusalem was led by the apostles. Eventually it became necessary for them to delegate some of their responsibilities to other mature Christian men. That enabled them to concentrate on prayer and teaching (v. 5).

Verse 1 says, "In those days, when the number of the disciples was multiplied, there arose a murmuring of the Grecians against the Hebrews, because their widows were neglected in the daily ministration." One of the church's responsibilities was to take care of widows. Contention arose because some Greek Christians thought that most of the daily provisions were going to the Jewish widows.

Therefore "the twelve called the multitude of the disciples unto them, and said, It is not fitting that we should leave the word of God, and serve tables" (v. 2). It was important that they concentrate on studying and communicating the Word of God. They understood what their priority was.

The apostles then said, "Wherefore, brethren, look among you for seven men of honest report, full of the Holy Spirit and wisdom, whom we may appoint over this business" (v. 3). The men were responsible for handing out financial support and various provisions to Christians in need. That way the apostles were able to give themselves "continually to prayer, and to the ministry of the word" (v. 4).

b) Their qualifications

First Timothy 3:8-9 gives some basic qualifications for deacons: "In like manner must the deacons be grave [serious minded], not double-tongued [telling one person one thing and another something else], not given to much wine, not greedy of filthy lucre, holding the mystery of the faith in a pure conscience." The "mystery of the faith" is that God and man are one in Jesus Christ (1 Tim. 3:16). Therefore "holding the mystery of the faith in a pure conscience" means living in a Christlike manner.

65

Furthermore, Paul said that deacons should "first be proved; then let them use the office of a deacon, being found blameless. . . . Let the deacons be the husbands of one wife, ruling their children and their own houses well. For they that have used the office of a deacon well purchase to themselves a good standing, and great boldness in the faith which is in Christ Jesus" (vv. 10, 12-13).

B. The Congregation They Lead

Whereas the basic task of the church leadership is teaching sound doctrine and explaining how to apply it, the basic task of the people is learning doctrine and then applying what they learn. The congregation is the object of the leaders' ministry. Perhaps someday, as a result of that ministry, members of the church will become deacons and deaconesses, elders, or even evangelists and pastor-teachers. We all start at the same point: somewhere in the congregation. Those who are faithful with small tasks can be entrusted with larger responsibilities. God may lift you to a place of leadership, possibly even to the point where you might be martyred for your faith in Jesus Christ.

1. General duties

The congregation is that part of the church that is to do "the work of the ministry" (Eph. 4:12). Hebrews 13:17 identifies the general obligation of the congregation: "Obey them that have the rule over you, and submit yourselves." Assuming that the leadership of the church is Spirit-led, we are to obey them because they are ministering on behalf of Christ, who is the Chief Shepherd (1 Pet. 5:4). The congregation is to subject itself to their godly ministry although they may not understand it all and may even disagree at times with what the elders are attempting to do. The church's obedience is a living testimony to the world.

Many things hurt a church and destroy its testimony. The primary one is poor leadership or false teachers who fail to build the church upon the Word of God. Another thing that weakens a church is a congregation that refuses to follow its leadership. That causes church splits as well as other problems that the world sees. Every church member must follow the design of the Spirit and be faithful and obedient.

The elders' duty is to provide instruction and loving care for the congregation, a burden for which they are answerable to God: "They watch for your souls, as they that must give account, that they may do it with joy, and not with grief; for that is unprofitable for you" (Heb. 13:17). It is difficult to rule the church of Christ and care about spiritual problems. Those who do are faced with problems twenty-four hours a day, seven days a week. Nevertheless leaders shouldn't have to labor in grief.

2. Specific duties

   a) Of the men

   What are the responsibilities of the men in a local assembly of Christians? Paul identified some of them for Timothy:

   (1) To their family

   First Timothy 5:8 says, "If any [man] provide not for his own [dependents], and specially for those of his own house, he hath denied the faith, and is worse than an [unbeliever]." If you can't show the world you are faithful to do your most basic duty, then you are denying the very basis of what Christian love is all about. There are times when men get laid off from work, but that should only be a temporary condition. God expects a Christian man to work so that he can provide for his family—he should not be on welfare unless he has some kind of physical incapacity. The church should care for a family in such a situation rather than allowing a mother with young children to support it.

(2) To their employer

    (*a*) 1 Timothy 6:1-2—"Let as many servants as are under the yoke count their own masters worthy of all honor, that the name of God and his doctrine be not blasphemed" (v. 1). Poor work habits discredit your Christian testimony. You need to serve your employer with honor whether he deserves it or not for the sake of how the world views Christianity.

    Verse 2 says, "They that have believing masters, let them not despise them because they are brethren." If you have a Christian boss, that doesn't mean you can goof off. Rather, "do them service because they are faithful and beloved, partakers of the benefit." That means you should work all the more diligently and not take advantage of his graciousness.

    (*b*) Titus 2:9-10—"Exhort servants to be obedient unto their own masters, and to please them well in all things, not answering again [talking back]; not purloining [stealing], but showing all good fidelity [honesty], that they may adorn the doctrine of God, our Savior, in all things." When you live a godly life in front of your employer, he will be able to see God manifest in your life and thus God will become more beautiful to him.

(3) To each other

    Titus 2:2 tells older men to be "sober-minded, grave, temperate, sound in faith, in love, in patience." Older men in the church are responsible to teach the younger ones. They should be serious, dignified, aware of their priorities, and self-controlled. They should also be strong in faith, love, and patience—attitudes directed toward God, others, and situations, respectively. Older men are to reflect many of the same qualities that the elders and deacons display in their lives.

Paul told Titus to exhort young men "to be sober-minded, in all things showing thyself a pattern of good works; in doctrine showing uncorruptness, gravity, sincerity, sound speech, that cannot be condemned" (vv. 6-8). It is easy for young men to say things that are not worth saying. They need to consider their words carefully before they speak. Young men are to be a pattern of God's standards. Paul told Timothy to be "an example [to] the believers" (1 Tim. 4:12).

(4) To God

First Timothy 2:8 says that men should "pray everywhere, lifting up holy hands, without wrath and doubting." Men are to be in constant prayer. That is an important reminder since it's so easy to be distracted by things of lesser importance.

b) Of the women

(1) To be modest

First Timothy 2:9 deals with a woman's clothing and appearance, which is as applicable today as when it was first established: "In like manner . . . women [should] adorn themselves in modest apparel." That is a basic principle for any believer, and the issue is modesty. The Bible doesn't say there is a three-inches-above-the-knee rule! But some things are obviously immodest.

Christians are to dress modestly, but that doesn't mean that if you bring to church an unsaved friend who is immodestly dressed the ushers are going to ask her to leave. The guideline in 1 Timothy is for believers.

(a) With godly fear

Women are to dress modestly "with godly fear [lit., "with a sense of shame"]" (v. 9). The modern idea that we don't need to be ashamed of our bodies is not biblical. Ever since sin came into the world, we have had a right to be ashamed of the corruptness of our flesh. Paul was not talking about extreme psychological trauma; he was saying that a woman—or a man for that matter—should have just enough shame to be modest.

(b) With sobriety

The idea of "sobriety" (v. 9) is to avoid extremes. There's no place in the church for showing off one's apparel. That distracts from what the Spirit of God wants to accomplish in our lives.

(c) Without fancy apparel

The end of verse 9 says that women should not adorn themselves "with braided hair, or gold, or pearls, or costly array." In Paul's day women wound all kinds of pearls and gold in their hair. You can imagine a man sitting in church with the rest of the believers when some lady sits down in front of him with a whole treasure chest on her head! He would be thinking how much her jewels were worth instead of worshiping God.

That doesn't mean Christian women can wear only cheap pearls and earrings. The point is that there's no place for a showy display in front of people who are trying to worship God. We are to be modestly attired so that we do not distract others from God's work through His Spirit and His Word. A Christian woman shouldn't adorn herself with immodest or extravagant apparel.

(d) With godly concerns

Verse 10 tells us that a godly woman is characterized by "good works." If you're a godly woman, you will look like someone who cares about godly things, not someone who cares only about showing off. A godly woman isn't concerned about putting herself on display.

(2) To learn in submission

First Timothy 2:11 says, "Let the women learn in silence with all subjection." Should the church have women preachers? No. That's exactly what that verse forbids. In the public service, women are not to teach. Verse 12 is even more specific: "I permit not a woman to teach, nor to usurp authority over the man, but to be in silence." There is no biblical justification for women preachers who lead and shepherd a congregation. However, the women in the church are more than welcome to teach other women and children (Titus 2:3-5; 1 Tim. 2:15).

(3) To live righteously

Titus 2:3 says older women should be "in behavior as becometh holiness, not false accusers." The Greek word translated "accusers" means "scandalmongers." It's easy for older people who have a lot of free time to get caught up in talking about what's going on, especially on the telephone. Information that begins as an innocent comment can become a real problem. Unfortunately, more churches have been split by scandals than any other single cause I can think of.

(4) To teach others

Women are to be "teachers of good things, that they may teach the young women to be sober-minded, to love their husbands, to love their children, to be discreet, chaste, keepers at home, good, obedient to their own husbands, that the word of God be not blasphemed" (Titus 2:3-4). The pastor is not responsible to teach everyone everything. That's the congregation's responsibility as God directs them to minister to others. Many young women wonder why their children resist discipline and have problems. One important reason is that many of these mothers are not home with their children and do not teach them spiritual principles that will become basic patterns for the rest of their lives. A godly woman will have her priorities in order, which means teaching her own children.

Focusing on the Facts

1. Why is it important to carefully evaluate someone's life before he can be put in a position of Christian leadership (see p. 60)?
2. What is the tragedy of the invisible church? Why does the church present a confusing picture to the world (see p. 60)?
3. Many churches today don't fit the biblical pattern of what they ought to be. Why not (see p. 61)?
4. What preparations do Paul and Barnabas make before selecting elders in Acts 14:21-23 (see p. 61)?
5. What two things does Paul encourage the Ephesian elders to do in Acts 20:28? Explain them (see p. 63).
6. Describe how Peter said that an elder should lead (1 Pet. 5:1-3; see p. 64).
7. What will elders receive who lead properly, according to 1 Peter 5:4 (see p. 64)?
8. To whom did the apostles delegate some of their responsibilities? Why (see p. 65)?
9. According to 1 Timothy 3:8-9, what are some of the basic qualifications for deacons (see p. 65)?
10. Compare the basic tasks of church leadership and the congregation (see p. 66).
11. What are the general duties of the congregation, according to Hebrews 13:17 (see p. 66)?
12. What are two things that hurt a church and destroy its testimony (see pp. 66-67)?
13. Why is a man who doesn't provide for his family's needs considered "worse than an [unbeliever]" (1 Tim. 5:8; see p. 67)?
14. How should Christian employees treat their employers? Why? If your boss is a Christian, how should you work (1 Tim. 6:1-2; see p. 68)?
15. How can a Christian employee "adorn the doctrine of God" (Titus 2:10; see p. 68)?

16. How should Christian women dress? Explain (see pp. 69-71).
17. Why should extreme clothing styles be avoided in church (see p. 70)?
18. What things should young women be taught, according to Titus 2:3-4? Who should be teaching them (see pp. 71-72)?

Pondering the Principles

1. If you are a Christian man, read Titus 1:5-9. Although you may not believe you are capable of serving as an elder, measure your life by the high biblical standards that are established for one. What weak areas do you need to strengthen to qualify you for service as a elder? Do you have a desire to be responsible for the spiritual nourishment of the church? Could your life be a suitable example to the believers in your church? Recognize that your faithful service now will be rewarded with "a crown of glory" from the chief Shepherd (1 Pet. 5:4).

2. Read Hebrews 13:17. How would you rate your submissiveness to the leaders of your church? Are you quick and willing to obey them, or is your resistance a cause of grief for them? Think of some things you could do that would bring joy to your church leaders. Be sure to implement them.

3. Review the Christian's responsibility to his employer (see p. 68). What type of relationship do you have with your supervisor, foreman, or employer? How do you honor him? Do you argue with him or privately resent his leadership? Have you ever prayed for him? Can he tell that you are a Christian by your work habits? If not, determine what you need to change so that your daily work can "adorn the doctrine of God" (Titus 2:10).

5
What God Wants the Church to Be

Outline

Introduction

Lesson
I. A Saved Church
   A. The Priority of the Church
      1. Exemplified
         a) Paul's strategy
         b) Paul's sermon
         c) The people's response
      2. Explained
      3. Evidenced
   B. The Purity of the Church
      1. The examples
         a) The church at Jerusalem
         b) The church at Pergamum
      2. The effects
II. A Surrendered Church
   A. Explained
   B. Exhorted
   C. Exemplified
III. A Suffering Church
   A. Recorded
   B. Reviewed
   C. Reinforced
IV. A Soul-Winning Church
   A. Living Exemplary Lives
   B. Proclaiming the Truth

Introduction

All the basic ingredients that our Lord wants in a church were found in the Thessalonian congregation. The epistle that Paul wrote to them shows us the kind of church that Christ builds. It contains no reference to the number of members. It doesn't tell us about their goals and objectives, their programming, the kind of sermons that were preached, or the music that they sang. It doesn't tell us about their Sunday school, their worship services, or their high school camps. However, it does tell us about several spiritual elements.

The apostle Paul first preached the gospel to the Thessalonians during his second missionary journey. After leaving them, he sent Timothy to find out how they were doing. When Timothy returned, he came with a fantastic report: "When Timothy came from you unto us, and brought us good tidings of your faith and love, and that ye have good remembrance of us always, desiring greatly to see us, as we also to see you; therefore, brethren, we were comforted" (1 Thess. 3:6-7). That good news prompted Paul to write his first letter to the Thessalonians.

I trust that as we look at some of the basic principles in the epistle to the Thessalonians, the Lord will help you see what He desires from you and how your church can be what He wants it to be. First Thessalonians gives a pattern for the ideal church.

Lesson

I. A SAVED CHURCH

A. The Priority of the Church

The church at Thessalonica was a saved church. That is significant because many churches today don't know the meaning of salvation. The Thessalonian church was an assembly of born-again Christians. That fact is verified in the first four verses of the book by the terms Paul used: "Paul, and Silvanus [Silas], and Timothy, unto the church of the Thessalonians which is in God, the Father, and in the Lord Jesus Christ: Grace be unto you, and peace, from God, our Father, and the Lord Jesus Christ. We give thanks to God always for you all, making mention of you in our prayers, remembering without ceasing your work of faith, and labor of love, and patience of hope in our Lord Jesus Christ, in the sight of God and our Father, knowing, brethren beloved, your election of God."

Paul could thank God for the Thessalonians because they were all "in the Lord Jesus Christ" (v. 1). They gave evidence of personally knowing Him as their Savior. Therein lies the beginning of an effective church. The reason so many churches are ineffective is the mixture of wheat and tares—even among the leadership. Having unregenerate people in places of responsibility works against what God is trying to accomplish, and confuses the church's message.

1. Exemplified

Let's look at Acts 17 to see how the church at Thessalonica began.

a) Paul's strategy

Verse 1 says, "When they had passed through Amphipolis and Apollonia, [Paul and his companions] came to Thessalonica, where was a synagogue of the

77

Jews." When Paul entered a city to spread the gospel, he generally went to the synagogue first because, being Jewish, he found his greatest opportunity there. Furthermore, he realized that if he went to the Gentiles first, the Jews would not be willing to listen to him.

b) Paul's sermon

Verses 2-3 report the content of Paul's preaching: "Paul, as his manner was, went in unto them, and three Sabbath days reasoned with them out of the scriptures, opening and alleging that Christ must needs have suffered, and risen again from the dead; and that this Jesus, whom I preach unto you, is Christ." The Jewish people had difficulty accepting Jesus as the Messiah because He had died. Most Jewish people did not understand the concept of a suffering Messiah, which was prophesied in such places as Isaiah 53 and Psalm 22. Therefore, Paul spent time showing them that the Messiah had to have suffered to fulfill God's plan. As a result of Paul's preaching, "some of them believed, and consorted with Paul and Silas; and of the devout Greeks a great multitude, and of the chief women not a few" (v. 4).

c) The people's response

From the very beginning, there was a tremendous response, even though Paul spent only three Sabbaths in Thessalonica. Paul was overjoyed to learn from Timothy that they were having a dynamic impact on the surrounding area.

2. Explained

Notice the phrases "in God, the Father, and in the Lord Jesus Christ" (v. 1), "in our Lord Jesus Christ" (v. 3), and "in the Holy Spirit" (v. 5). Paul used the phrase "in Christ" in his epistles 132 times. It identifies the relationship that believers have with the living God. We don't just follow the teachings of Christ—we are *in* Christ.

a) 1 Corinthians 6:17—"He that is joined unto the Lord is one spirit."

b) Romans 6:3-5, 8—Paul said this regarding the identity of a believer in his union with Christ: "Know ye not that, as many of us as were baptized into Jesus Christ [placed into union with him] were baptized into His death? Therefore, we are buried with him by baptism into death, that as Christ was raised up from the dead by the glory of the Father, even so we also should walk in newness of life. For if we have been planted together in the likeness of his death, we shall be also in the likeness of his resurrection. . . . Now if we be dead with Christ, we believe that we shall also live with him."

Paul was not referring to water baptism, although that does symbolize the spiritual realities of death with Christ and new life in Him. The act of baptism is not a saving act. He was merely saying that when you became a Christian, you were placed in the church of Jesus Christ by a divine miracle. Your old life died, and you rose to walk in newness of life in His resurrection. Therefore, you are inextricably linked in union with Jesus Christ.

c) Galatians 2:20—Paul said, "I am crucified with Christ: nevertheless I live; yet not I, but Christ liveth in me." The Christian experience is not simply following the moral precepts of a man or believing in a historical figure; instead, it is believers experiencing union with the living God through Jesus Christ.

d) 2 Corinthians 5:17—What are the results of being in Christ? "If any man be in Christ, he is a new creation." When you come into union with Christ, you become a new creation because the old self dies and you are made new.

e) 1 Thessalonians 2:13—Paul thanked God for the Thessalonians because they so readily received His truth: "For this cause also thank we God without ceasing because, when ye received the word of God which ye heard of us, ye received it, not as the word of men but as it is in truth, the Word of God, which effectually worketh also in you that believe." They didn't receive Paul's preaching as some philosophy or new theology. When they heard the Word, they realized it wasn't just something to tickle their intellect or give them a new religious experience. They were regenerated internally as a result of receiving and believing the gospel.

f) 2 Peter 1:4—It is an incredible privilege to be a Christian; the very life of God is yours! Peter said believers have become "partakers of the divine nature."

3. Evidenced

Paul began 1 Thessalonians by saying, "Grace be unto you, and peace, from God, our Father, and the Lord Jesus Christ" because the Thessalonians were receiving those blessings. No one can receive the grace or peace of God unless he is a child of God. So even the beginning of Paul's letter acknowledges the salvation of the Thessalonians.

The evidence of their salvation is also indicated in verse 3: "[We remember] without ceasing your work of faith, and labor of love, and patience of hope." That mighty combination of Christian virtues—faith, hope, and love—belongs only to the redeemed. As a result of what he saw in the lives of the Thessalonians, Paul knew they were redeemed. There weren't any phonies in Thessalonica—they were a pure congregation.

B. The Purity of the Church

The purity of the church is a prerequisite to effectively serving God. Since God blesses a church that is saved, we know that Satan wants to infiltrate churches with unbelievers—especially at high levels. How do you keep unbelievers out of the church? It is not easy—it is difficult to distinguish wheat from tares. In fact, Jesus cautioned against trying to separate false believers from true ones. We must wait for Him to do that in the end times (Matt. 13:27-30).

1. The examples

    a) The church at Jerusalem

        Ananias and Sapphira apparently envied the praise others received for having given to those in need. So they decided to sell a piece of property and give the proceeds to the Lord. However, they decided to keep a little, thinking no one would ever find out. As a result, the Lord caused them to drop dead in front of the congregation (Acts 5:1-5, 10).

        Such serious and sudden discipline had a profound effect. Everyone in that congregation probably adjusted anything that wasn't right immediately. In fact verses 11-13 say, "Great fear came upon all the church, and upon as many as heard these things. . . . And of the rest dared no man join himself to them." The word spread throughout Jerusalem not to join that organization because just one mistake resulted in death! The realization that sin will be dealt with deters the tares from mixing with the wheat.

    b) The church at Pergamum

        Revelation 2:14 records Christ's warning against having a congregation filled with unbelievers. To the church of Pergamum He said, "I have a few things against thee, because thou hast there them that hold the doctrine of Balaam." He was referring to compromise with the world's system. Balaam was instrumental in causing Israel to interact sinfully with pagans (Num. 31:15-16). In Revelation 2:16 Jesus says, "Repent, or else I will come unto thee quickly, and will fight against them with the sword of my mouth." Christ will purge His church if it compromises with the world and begins to allow intermarriage with the system.

2. The effects

    The key to the success of the Thessalonian church was its purity. Acts 2 tells us three thousand people believed the gospel and were baptized at the birth of the church on the day of Pentecost. Verse 41 says "they continued steadfastly." That regenerated church turned the city of Jerusalem upside down. They made such an impact that the Jewish leaders said, "Ye have filled Jerusalem with your doctrine" (Acts 5:28). When you have a totally regenerated assembly of people moving through town in the power of the Holy Spirit, they are bound to make a great impact.

It was no different for the Thessalonians. Paul said, "Our gospel came not unto you in word only, but also in power, and in the Holy Spirit, and in much assurance, as ye know what manner of men we were among you for your sake" (1 Thess. 1:5). When the Thessalonians received and believed the gospel, they experienced the energy of the Holy Spirit and the assurance and transformation that accompanies union with Christ.

II. A SURRENDERED CHURCH

A. Explained

Verse 6 of chapter 1 says, "Ye became followers of us, and of the Lord." The genuine character of their salvation is apparent in that statement. The Greek word translated "followers" is *mimētēs*, from which the English word *mimic* is derived. The Thessalonian Christians weren't just talkers; they were imitators. They didn't merely talk about their Christian experience; they actually modeled their lives after Paul and his companions.

B. Exhorted

Imitating godly men was a constant theme of Paul's.

1. 1 Corinthians 4:16—"Wherefore, I beseech you, be ye followers of me." Paul didn't have to say that to the Thessalonians because they were already doing it.

2. 1 Corinthians 11:1—It may seem audacious that Paul told people to pattern their lives after his, but not when we consider the Christlikeness of his life. He told the Corinthians, "Be ye followers of me, even as I also am of Christ."

In Ephesians 5:1 Paul says, "Be ye, therefore, followers of God." Paul exhorted Christians to be followers of God, Christ, and himself. That is precisely what was happening in the Thessalonian assembly. They were committed to being like Jesus.

C. Exemplified

Christians are to be not only collective representatives of Christ on earth but also individual representatives as each believer strives to be like Him. The pursuit of the Christian is to be like Christ. That's the key to unity in the church. If all of us are like Christ, we will have no problem in getting along with each other.

Unfortunately, we are not always in tune with one another because we are not all following Christ. A. W. Tozer said that if a hundred pianos were tuned to each other, their pitch would not be very accurate. But if they were all tuned to one tuning fork, they would automatically be tuned to each other. Similarly, unity in the church isn't the result of adjusting to everyone else. Rather, it is becoming like Jesus Christ. The Thessalonian church was surrendered to Christlikeness, which had been demonstrated in the lives of Paul, Silas, and Timothy.

III. A SUFFERING CHURCH

First Thessalonians 1:6 says, "Ye became followers of us, and of the Lord, having received the word in much affliction, with joy of the Holy Spirit." The Thessalonian church didn't have it easy. In fact, any church that is saved and surrendered to Christ is going to have a difficult time.

A. Recorded

As soon as the Thessalonian assembly began, they experienced opposition. Acts 17 records what happened: "The Jews who believed not, moved with envy, took unto them certain vile fellows of the baser sort, and gathered a company, and set all the city in an uproar, and assaulted the house of Jason, and sought to bring [Paul, Silas, and Timothy] out to the people. And when they found them not, they drew Jason and certain brethren unto the rulers of the city, crying, These that have turned the world upside down are come here also" (vv. 5-6). Persecution began immediately for that church.

B. Reviewed

First Thessalonians 2:14-16 reviews the persecution that the church had experienced: "Ye, brethren, became followers of the churches of God which in Judea are in Christ Jesus; for ye also have suffered like things of your own countrymen, even as they have of the Jews, who both killed the Lord Jesus and their own prophets, and have persecuted us; and they please not God, and are contrary to all men, forbidding us to speak to the Gentiles that they might be saved, to fill up their sins always; for the wrath is come upon them to the uttermost."

C. Reinforced

The church that is saved and surrendered to Christ antagonizes the world. Consequently suffering will come. Jesus said, "If the world hate you, ye know that it hated me before it hated you. . . . If they have persecuted me, they will also persecute you" (John 15:18, 20).

In Colossians 1:24 we read that Paul was willing to suffer if it brought about the salvation of others: "[I] rejoice in my sufferings for you, and fill up that which is behind of the afflictions of Christ in my flesh." Paul meant that since the world couldn't directly persecute Jesus anymore, it would persecute His followers instead. The apostle was willing to suffer for the One who had suffered for him.

Wouldn't it be great to be persecuted for being Christlike because you've turned the world upside down? If unbelievers became irritated about your church (assuming it wasn't for being unnecessarily offensive), it would probably mean that the church was correctly preaching the gospel in a manner that exposes sin. The church that confronts the world is going to suffer. Tradition records that eleven out of the twelve apostles were martyred.

The Conscience of the World

The church is to be the conscience of the world. It must confront sin without being obnoxious and earning a bad reputation. That's not to say we should be unkind to people who don't know Christ. Rather the opposite should be true. When the world is sinful, we need to expose its sin. When the world needs a clear picture of Christ, we want to present that picture. And when Satan and his system opposes the truth, we need to be ready. The church needs to be in the world but not a part of the world (John 17:15-18). We function as its conscience by helping people face the realities of God, Christ, sin, death, and immortality.

IV. A SOUL-WINNING CHURCH

A. Living Exemplary Lives

The Thessalonian church had a marvelous twofold testimony. First they spread the gospel by living exemplary lives. Paul said of them, "Ye were an example to all that believe in Macedonia and Achaia" (1 Thess. 1:7). Other people could look at the Thessalonian church and be attracted to Christ by what they saw. Amazingly, it took the Thessalonians only two weeks to establish life-styles that were surrendered to Christ.

The Thessalonians were like Jesus Christ. They set a pattern for everyone else, including believers. Chapter 1 shows the response that believers in Macedonia and Achaia had as a result of the Thessalonians' testimony: "They themselves show of us what manner of entering in we had unto you, and how ye turned to God from idols, to serve the living and true God" (v. 9).

Paul didn't have to tell others about the conversion of the Thessalonians because they spread the news with their lives. The latest news was that many people in Thessalonica had turned to God from idols. Incredibly, Thessalonica was only fifty miles from Mount Olympus—the supposed residence of the Greek gods. Although the people had been reared from their earliest years to believe in a plurality of gods, within three successive Sabbaths an entire community of believers dropped their idolatrous system and began serving the living God. That kind of turnaround makes news.

We first witness to the world by our transformed lives. For example, if you are a drunk, you can't help a drunkard by telling him to shape up. If you are a crook, you can't help another crook by telling him to be an honest man. If you are living an ungodly life, you don't have anything to offer people.

B. Proclaiming the Truth

The second way of spreading the gospel is through a verbal witness of the Word. First Thessalonians 1:8 says, "From you sounded out the word of the Lord . . . in every place." The Greek word translated "sounded out" is *exēchētai,* from which we get the English word *echo.* One's Christian testimony should never be independent of God's Word. It should be only an echo of God's truth. An echo always repeats what was originally spoken. God has put His voice, the Holy Spirit, in you. He doesn't want you to create your own words; He wants you to echo His truth.

The Thessalonian congregation led such exemplary lives that the world couldn't believe it. The dramatic transformation of their characters created a platform of credibility from which they echoed "the word of the Lord not only in Macedonia and Achaia, but also in every place" (v. 8). As a result, Paul explained that he and his companions didn't need to tell anyone the gospel because the Thessalonian congregation had already spread the news everywhere.

How did the news get around so fast if 1 Thessalonians was only written a short time after the church was started? The city of Thessalonica was located on the Via Egnatia, the main east-west highway. It was a major land trade route. The city, located on the Thermaic Gulf, was a seaport that served as a hub of commerce. Before long, the news had spread and everyone was talking about the little assembly in Thessalonica that not only lived the gospel but preached it as well.

V. A SECOND-COMING CHURCH

Verse 10 says the Thessalonians turned from idols to serve God "and to wait for his Son from heaven, whom he raised from the dead, even Jesus, who delivered us from the wrath to come." Jesus promised He would come back and gather the faithful to be with Him forever (John 14:1-3). Consequently the ideal church awaits His return.

A. The Mockers

Did you know that many churches aren't waiting for Christ's return? Peter said, "There shall come in the last days scoffers, walking after their own lusts, and saying, Where is the promise of His coming?" (2 Pet. 3:3-4). There are people today who claim to be Christians, but don't ever talk about the return of Christ. In fact, I heard a preacher say, "I never talk about the return of Christ— there's too much confusion on that issue." Maybe it's fortunate for his congregation that he doesn't. There's no sense in adding more confusion to that which already exists. But that doesn't excuse him from speaking the truth. Every church that is truly committed to being what God wants must be aware that Jesus is coming back.

B. The Motivation

Anticipation of Christ's return should motivate us to live godly lives for His service in the present.

1. The rewards

The last recorded words of Jesus are: "Behold, I come quickly, and my reward is with me, to give every man according as his work shall be" (Rev. 22:12). The only way you can prove that you love Him is to serve Him with your whole heart. Then at His return you will receive "gold, silver, [and] precious stones" instead of "wood, hay, [and] stubble" (1 Cor. 3:12). According to Revelation 4:10 we will cast our crowns, which are symbolic of rewards, at His feet. The more crowns you have earned, the more you can give back to Him.

2. The responsibility

Knowing that Christ is coming again should give us a
sense of urgency about sharing the good news with
others. After His resurrection, Jesus said, "Ye shall receive power, after the Holy Spirit is come upon you;
and ye shall be witnesses unto me," (Acts 1:8). When
He had ascended into heaven, two angels appeared
and said, "This same Jesus, who is taken up from you
into heaven, shall so come in like manner as ye have
seen him go into heaven" (v. 11). Paul says in 2 Corinthians 5:11, "Knowing, therefore, the terror of the
Lord, we persuade men." When I realize the impending judgment of God, I can't help but persuade men
and women to be "reconciled to God" (v. 20).

A church that doesn't believe in the return of Jesus Christ
has no sense of rewards or urgency to deliver the ungodly
from judgment. However, the Lord wants us to remember
His return.

VI. A STEADFAST CHURCH

A. Explained

First Thessalonians 3:8 says, "For now we live, if ye stand
fast in the Lord." Standing fast in the Lord means two
things: not wavering doctrinally, and maintaining a steadfast love. A person can stand fast doctrinally but dry up
spiritually. That's why a Christian needs to stand fast in
terms of love.

Unfortunately the church at Ephesus didn't. Our Lord re-
proved them, saying, "I have somewhat against thee, because thou hast left thy first love" (Rev. 2:4). The
Ephesians were correct doctrinally, but they failed to have
both ingredients of a healthy church—sound doctrine and
love. When you stand firm on the Word of God without
wavering and in a commitment of love to one another,
you've got a strong stand.

B. Exemplified

1. By their sound doctrine

The Thessalonian church stood firmly on the Word of God. Paul said, "Our gospel came not unto you in word only, but also in power, and in the Holy Spirit. . . . And ye became followers of us, and of the Lord, having received the word in much affliction" (1:5-6). Paul also told them, "Ye received the word of God . . . not as the word of men but as it is in truth, the word of God" (2:13). "We were comforted over you in all our affliction and distress by your faith" (3:7). How exciting it is when a church doesn't waver from its doctrine or from its commitment to love one another!

I often pray that God will help our church continue to stand true to His Word—especially since Satan wants to infiltrate the church with "grievous wolves" (Acts 20:29) who will devour the saints. God wants us to be aware that false teachers can arise from within the church. Therefore, we must be committed to standing fast in sound doctrine. I've talked to pastors who have left their churches because they had fallen into false doctrine. That is heartbreaking because those pastors were responsible for leading some of their members to Christ. Two things could break my heart: if Grace church lost its firm stand on doctrine and if the congregation stopped loving one another.

2. By their steadfast love

The Thessalonians stood fast in love. Paul said, "As touching brotherly love, ye need not that I write unto you; for ye yourselves are taught of God to love one another. And, indeed, ye do it toward all the brethren" (4:9-10). Paul didn't need to say much about the quality of their love because they were faithfully putting it into practice.

VII. A SUBMISSIVE CHURCH

A. Explained

This final principle isn't as obvious as the others. In no other New Testament epistle did Paul make as many unqualified and undefended commands as he did in this one. For example, when Paul wrote to the Corinthians he repeatedly defended his instructions (e.g., 1 Cor. 1:10–2:5; 2 Cor. 10:1–13:10).

B. Exemplified

However, Paul didn't have to reprimand or convince the Thessalonians of anything. In chapter 4 he says, "Study to be quiet, and to do your own business, and to work with your own hands, as we commanded you" (v. 11). Similarly, chapter 5 contains many brief, unqualified commands: "We beseech you, brethren, to know them who labor among you, and are over you in the Lord, and admonish you, and to esteem them very highly in love for their work's sake. And be at peace among yourselves. Now we exhort you, brethren, warn them that are unruly, encourage the fainthearted, support the weak, be patient toward all men. See that none render evil for evil unto any man, but ever follow that which is good, both among yourselves, and to all men. Rejoice evermore. Pray without ceasing. In everything give thanks; for this is the will of God in Christ Jesus concerning you. Quench not the Spirit. Despise not prophesyings. Prove all things; hold fast that which is good. Abstain from all appearance of evil" (vv. 12-22).

Paul didn't need to give a detailed explanation of his instructions to the Thessalonians because they obviously were a submissive church. He didn't have to defend himself. Imagine a preacher getting up on Sunday morning and saying only, "My text for this morning is 1 Thessalonians 5:16—'Rejoice evermore!' Now let us pray. Next week we'll look at verse 17." If Paul said to the Corinthians, "Pray without ceasing," he would have needed three chapters to explain why he said that! But that wasn't necessary with the Thessalonian church.

Paul said, "Ye became followers of us, and of the Lord, having received the word in much affliction, with joy" (1:6). In the next chapter he said, "Ye received the word of God . . . not as the word of men but as it is in truth, the word of God" (2:13). And in chapter 4 he said, "Furthermore, then, we beseech you, brethren, and exhort you by the Lord Jesus, that as ye have received of us how ye ought to walk and to please God" (v. 1). The Thessalonians unconditionally submitted to the Word of God.

The Primary Role of a Pastor

The primary role of a pastor is to teach his people to submit to Scripture. If a pastor preaches on topics that are purely his own ideas without any biblical content, that church will not be trained to accept the Word of God when it is presented. Should a problem arise in the church, the pastor might feel the need to preach a biblical sermon. However, the people will probably be indifferent toward that since they have not already learned to submit to the Word. To them Scripture will merely sound like more of their pastor's opinions. The biblical pastor leads his church to receive and obey the Word willingly.

Focusing on the Facts

1. Why did Paul send Timothy back to Thessalonica? What did Timothy report about the church in that city (see p. 76)?
2. Why could Paul thank God for the Thessalonians (see p. 77)?
3. Why are many churches ineffective? What is the result of having unbelieving people in places of responsibility within the church (see p. 77)?
4. Why did Paul preach in the synagogues first when he arrived at a city (see p. 78)?
5. According to Acts 17:2-3, what was Paul's message to the Thessalonian Jews (see p. 78)?
6. What does it mean to be "in the Lord Jesus Christ" (1 Thess. 1:1; see p. 78)?
7. What evidence did Paul cite that demonstrated the salvation of the Thessalonians (see p. 80)?
8. What is a prerequisite for a church to effectively serve God (see p. 80)?

9. Of whom did the Thessalonians become followers? Why (see p. 82)?
10. What is the key to unity in the church? Explain (see p. 83).
11. Describe the opposition the Thessalonian church experienced (see pp. 83-84).
12. Why does the world persecute Christians (John 15:18, 20; see p. 84)?
13. Why was Paul willing to suffer for Christ (see p. 84)?
14. How can the church be the conscience of the world (see p. 85)?
15. Why didn't Paul have to tell surrounding cities about the conversion of the Thessalonians (see pp. 85-86)?
16. How did the Thessalonians spread the gospel (see p. 86)?
17. How should the anticipation of Christ's return motivate us (see p. 87)?
18. What should Christ's return give us a sense of urgency about (see p. 88)?
19. In what two complementary things does a Christian need to stand fast (see p. 88)?
20. What happens when sound doctrine is not balanced with love? Give a biblical example of a church that failed to keep that balance (see p. 88).
21. Why was it apparently not necessary for Paul to defend his commands before the Thessalonians (see p. 90)?
22. What is a submissive church eager to receive and obey (1 Thess. 2:13; see p. 91)?

Pondering the Principles

1. Meditate on Ephesians 4:13, 24; Hebrews 12:10; and 1 John 3:2-3. Praise God that He has enabled us as Christians to become "partakers of the divine nature" (2 Pet. 1:4).

2. Are you a follower of godly Christians, as the Thessalonians were? To determine the kind of people you should pattern your life after, read Titus 1:5–2:15. If such examples are currently lacking in your church, strive to become one yourself so that others may follow you. As you systematically read through the New Testament, study the life of Christ and the supreme example He has set for you.

3. Evaluate yourself and the spiritual health of your church on the basis of the seven characteristics we've seen in the Thessalonian church. Have you and the majority of your church been saved? Are you committed to being like Christ, and are you willing to suffer for Him? Are you regularly praying for opportunities to share the gospel? Are you living the kind of life that will lend credence to your message? Does your church have a ministry for training people to evangelize? Are you anxiously awaiting the return of Christ? Does your church share the same sense of urgency that the Thessalonian church did? Does your church have a proper balance of love and sound doctrine? Are you submissive to the leaders of your church, or are you often indifferent or in opposition to what they are trying to accomplish? If any of those elements are lacking in your life or in your church, determine what steps you can take to strengthen those areas.

6
The Calling of the Church

Outline

Introduction
A. The Calling of the Church Explained
B. The Calling of the Church Expressed

Lesson
  I. Called Before: Election (vv. 4-5, 11)
     A. A Temporal Context
     B. A Tremendous Confidence
 II. Called out: Redemption (vv. 7, 13)
     A. Stated
     B. Related
III. Called from: Sanctification (v. 4)
     A. The Requirement
     B. The Responsibility
 IV. Called to: Identification (vv. 4-6)
     A. Stated
     B. Supported
  V. Called Under: Revelation (vv. 7-9)
     A. The Practical Content of Revelation
     B. The Personal Commitment to Revelation
 VI. Called with: Unification (v. 10)
VII. Called unto: Glorification (v. 11)
VIII. Called for: Proclamation (v. 6)

Introduction

Grace Community Church is unique. It has been the subject of much discussion throughout the years among pastors, church leaders, laymen, and even secular authorities. Magazines have written articles about us. Doctoral students have written theses on our church. Many reports have tried to analyze us. We have been dissected, examined, studied, labeled, categorized, scrutinized, copied, blessed, cursed, defended, ignored, endowed, publicized, and even sued. What has caused all that attention?

The key to understanding Grace church is not in analyzing its pastors, staff, programs, methods, elders, congregation, growth, size, or location. All those things are essential to what we are, but the real key is revealed in our very name—Grace Community *Church*. The world has such a difficult time understanding us because it doesn't understand what a church is. The term *church* sets us and all other true churches apart from other human institutions. We have been purchased with Christ's own blood. No other institution in the world owes its existence to that fact.

A. The Calling of the Church Explained

Unfortunately the word *church* has lost its profound richness. Today it brings to mind a building of bricks and mortar on some corner. Some think of the church as an institutional hierarchy of religious orders.

To understand what the church is, we need to look at its Greek counterpart. "Church" is a translation of the Greek word *ekklēsia*. The term is derived from the verb root *kaleō*, which means "to call." That is a good definition of the church: we are *the called*. In fact, Romans 8:28 wonderfully defines the assembly of believers as "the called according to his purpose." We are a group summoned together by God for His purpose. We are not a human organization. We are not the result of man's ingenuity or power. We were not built by good, religious people. Rather, we have been called by God into existence.

B. The Calling of the Church Expressed

That it is God who calls believers is emphasized throughout the New Testament:

1. Romans 1:6-7—Paul, writing to the church at Rome, said, "Among whom are ye also the called of Jesus

Christ; to all that be in Rome, beloved of God, called to be saints."

2. 1 Corinthians 1:2—"Unto the church of God which is at Corinth, to them that are sanctified in Christ Jesus, called to be saints, with all that in every place shall call upon the name of Jesus Christ, our Lord."

3. 1 Corinthians 1:26—"Ye see your calling, brethren." Paul described the character of those who make up the church.

4. Ephesians 4:1, 4—"Walk worthy of the vocation to which ye are called. . . . Ye are called in one hope of your calling."

5. 1 Thessalonians 2:12—"Walk worthy of God, who hath called you unto his kingdom and glory."

6. 2 Timothy 1:9—"[God] hath saved us, and called us with an holy calling, not according to our works, but according to his own purpose and grace."

7. 1 Peter 5:10—"The God of all grace . . . who hath called us unto his eternal glory by Christ Jesus."

The entire church has been called into existence by God Himself. It doesn't exist because of the genius of man, the charisma of leaders, the power of persuasive speech, the affluence of members, the effectiveness of its facilities, the wisdom of its committees, or the hard work of its members. It is ultimately the work of God. The true church is led by God's Spirit through God's Word in the lives of obedient people.

That helps to explain the church's overall success and blessing. However, it has weaknesses and failures because God has chosen to work through human agencies. When we succeed it is because of Him, not us. When we fail it is because of us, not Him. The main goal of the church is to let God work and build His kingdom as we obediently submit to His Word and His Spirit. Ephesians 1 helps us to understand the extent of what it means to be called by Him to do just that.

I. CALLED BEFORE: Election (vv. 4-5, 11)

"He hath chosen us in him before the foundation of the world . . . having predestinated us unto the adoption of sons by Jesus Christ to himself, according to the good pleasure of his will . . . being predestinated according to the purpose of him who worketh all things after the counsel of his own will."

A. A Temporal Context

The church did not accidentally come into being. It is the result of God's predetermined, sovereign call.

The apostle Paul reiterates God's election in 2 Timothy 1:9: "[God has] saved us, and called us with an holy calling, not according to our works, but according to his own purpose and grace, which was given us in Christ Jesus before the world began."

In the hymn "The Inner Life," an anonymous lyricist wrote,

> I sought the Lord and afterwards I knew
> He moved my soul to seek Him, seeking me.
> It was not I that found O Savior true.
> No, I was found by Thee.

The church is fulfilling a predetermined destiny, a calling from beyond space and time. In God's mind, there is no time frame. Everything is an immediate eternal present. The church was as real to Him before the world began as it is now. God continues to add to the church those whom He predetermined would believe in Christ.

B. A Tremendous Confidence

That should give us a tremendous sense of confidence. Before I came to Grace church, I was a pastoral candidate for a large, well-known church. However, the leaders there concluded that I was too young and inexperienced for their church. Although I was open to wherever the Lord wanted me to go, I was disappointed. But God's plan wasn't for me to be there; it was for me to be at Grace church. Before the foundation of the world, God knew that He would use Grace church to redeem souls and that I would be a part of that process. It thrills me every time I hear about someone's being saved in our church because it is one more example of the fulfillment of God's predestined plan.

People aren't saved by accident; the Lord is building His church. That takes tremendous pressure off me because I don't have to build the church. Years ago a reporter asked me, "Do you have a great desire to build the church?" I said, "I have no desire to build the church because Christ said He would build the church, and I certainly don't want to compete with Him. I just want to be a part of what He's building."

Grace church is Christ's church. Consequently, there's no sense of panic or frustration in my ministry. There's no reason to seek worldly means to get results. All we need to do is rest in the Spirit of God and be faithful to commit our lives to Christ. He will surely build His church.

II. CALLED OUT: Redemption (vv. 7, 13)

"In [Christ] we have redemption through his blood, the forgiveness of sins, according to the riches of his grace . . . in whom ye also trusted, after ye heard the word of truth, the gospel of your salvation; in whom also after ye believed, ye were sealed with that Holy Spirit of promise."

A. Stated

Paul identified the church as those who have been graciously redeemed and forgiven. God has "delivered us from the power of darkness, and hath translated us into the kingdom of his dear Son" (Col. 1:13). We have been called out of sin, death, and the world's system into life (Rom. 6:8-11; 1 John 2:15-17). We are a redeemed community, born again by the Spirit of God. That is the only reason we are part of the true church. If we weren't redeemed, we wouldn't be a church in the truest sense of the word.

Unredeemed people who assemble under a religious banner with a title of "church" are not part of the church that Christ is building. There are so-called churches all over the world that appear to be alive but are dead (Rev. 3:1). Rather than being called out from the world, they are part of it—in spite of their religious exercises.

B. Related

Having a church congregation that is truly saved is so important to me that I preached on that subject the first Sunday I was at Grace church. My text was Matthew 7:21-23: "Not every one that saith unto me, Lord, Lord, shall enter into the kingdom of heaven. . . . Many will say to me in that day, Lord, Lord, have we not prophesied in thy name? . . . And then will I profess unto them, I never knew you; depart from me." Perhaps you think I should have waited before I hit them between the eyes with a message such as that! But I was concerned that people were present who thought they were part of the church but really were not.

A church needs to understand from the very beginning what it is, so that it can know what direction it should be going. As a result of that confrontive sermon, several couples left the church, and we discovered that at least one elder was not a Christian. A church must do its best to distinguish between the wheat and the tares, the true and the false, those who *play* church and those who *are* the church.

How to Play Church

The title of my first sermon was "How to Play Church." In Luke 6:46 Jesus says, "Why call ye me, Lord, Lord, and do not the things which I say?" Reminiscent of that verse is a painting in the cathedral of Lübeck, Germany, entitled "The Lament of Jesus Christ Against the Ungrateful World." The corresponding text reads,

You call Me master, and obey Me not;
You call Me light, and see Me not;
You call Me the way, and walk Me not;
You call Me life, and live Me not;
You call Me wise, and follow Me not;
You call Me fair, and love Me not;
You call Me rich, and ask Me not;
You call Me eternal, and seek Me not.
If I condemn thee, blame Me not.

He Knew the Shepherd

I read about an old pastor who had been forced to retire because years of preaching had caused his voice to crack. Although a humble man, he was invited to a high-society luncheon by a friend.

The person heading up the luncheon requested a famous actor who was present to recite something for the guests. Agreeing to do so, he asked if anyone had a specific request. The old pastor thought for a moment and said, "How about the Twenty-third Psalm?" The actor replied, "That's an unusual request, but I happen to know it. I'll do it on one condition, though: you recite it after me." The old pastor hadn't bargained for that, but for the sake of the Lord, he agreed.

The actor stood up and recited the Twenty-third Psalm with the great intonation of his lyrical voice. When he finished, everyone applauded. The old pastor then stood and went through the psalm in his humble way with a cracking voice. When he was done, there was not a dry eye in the room. Sensing the emotion of the moment, the actor said, "You clapped for me, but you wept for him. The difference is obvious: I know the psalm, but he knows the Shepherd."

If there's one thing that a church must be, it is an assembly of people who know the Shepherd.

III. CALLED FROM: Sanctification (v. 4)

"That we should be holy and without blame before him."

A. The Requirement

As Christians, we have been called from the world to pursue holiness. First Peter 1:16 says, "Be ye holy; for I am holy." We are called to be separated from the world. We are to be uncompromising. The Spirit has instructed us to keep ourselves "unspotted from the world" (James 1:27). The Lord desires a church "not having spot, or wrinkle, or any such thing; but that it should be holy and without blemish" (Eph. 5:27). Paul's desire was to present the church "as a chaste virgin to Christ" (2 Cor. 11:2). God has called us to holiness, Christlikeness, and virtue.

B. The Responsibility

Christians are to manifest the holiness of our heavenly Father, our Savior, and the Spirit who dwells within us. We are to separate ourselves from complicity with the world (2 Cor. 6:17). We are not to practice the deeds of the flesh (Gal. 5:16-25; Col. 3:5). First John 2:15 warns us not to love the world's system, which is opposed to God. We have been called to holy lives. Therefore as a church we must emphasize the importance of humility, the confession of sin, church discipline, and worship of a holy God so we might live in reverential fear of Him.

When a group is unholy, they may call themselves a church, but they are not a true church unless they address the issue of sin. Show me a church that doesn't preach on sin, and I'll show you a church full of unholiness. The church must not tolerate unholiness. A pastor can't preach against sin yet do nothing about it. Otherwise people will think that biblical instruction and everyday living are unrelated. A church must seek holiness in the lives of its leaders as well as in the lives of its followers.

First Thessalonians 5:23-24 is a call to holiness: "The very God of peace sanctify you wholly; and I pray God your whole spirit and soul and body be preserved blameless unto the coming of our Lord Jesus Christ. Faithful is he that calleth you, who also will do it." In our pursuit of holiness, we must first recognize the holiness of God and Christ that we might appropriately fear them. In the gospel accounts, people often feared Jesus when His glory and His holiness were revealed to them (Mark 9:5-6; Luke 5:8).

We are uniquely called according to God's purpose, and part of that purpose is to be holy.

IV. CALLED TO: Identification (vv. 4-6)

"He hath chosen us in him . . . that we should be holy and without blame before him, in love having predestinated us unto the adoption of sons by Jesus Christ to himself. . . . He hath made us accepted in the Beloved."

A. Stated

The prepositional phrases "in him," "before him," "to himself," and "in the Beloved" reveal that Christians are intimately identified with God and Christ.

B. Supported

1. 1 Thessalonians 1:1—This epistle begins, "Paul, and Silvanus, and Timothy, unto the church of the Thessalonians which is in God, the Father, and in the Lord Jesus Christ." The church is called to an intimate identification with God Himself.

2. 1 John 1:3—Our personal union with God is a marvelous fellowship. According to John, "Our fellowship is with the Father, and with his Son, Jesus Christ."

3. John 17:22—Before His arrest, Jesus prayed that believers might be one with Him as He and the Father are one.

4. 1 Corinthians 6:17—"He that is joined unto the Lord is one spirit."

5. Romans 8:14-17—Christians have become intimately related to God, having been adopted as His sons. That makes us joint heirs with Christ. The church isn't a group you join by signing your name. It isn't some

kind of society merely committed to a system of teaching.

6. Romans 6:4-5—When we were saved, we entered into a personal relationship with the living God through Jesus Christ. We are identified with Christ in His death, and raised with Him in His resurrection so that we might "walk in newness of life" (v. 4).

7. Galatians 2:20—Paul said, "I am crucified with Christ: nevertheless I live; yet not I, but Christ liveth in me." That is a clear statement of the believer's spiritual union with Christ. In my own life I don't know where John MacArthur ends and Jesus Christ begins. (But when I sin, I know that I am responsible!) Like Paul, I have been "crucified with Christ . . . and the life which I now live in the flesh I live by the faith of the Son of God." The life of Christ and your own life should be so intertwined that you can't differentiate between them. It should be natural for you to see God at work in your life, sensing His power, experiencing His answers to your prayers, following His guidance, and being refreshed by His comfort.

We don't believe God is some cosmic ogre waiting to step on us if we break one of His rules. Rather, we have an intimate love relationship with Him.

V. CALLED UNDER: Revelation (vv. 7-9)

"In whom we have redemption through his blood, the forgiveness of sins, according to the riches of his grace, in which he hath abounded toward us in all wisdom and prudence, having made known unto us the mystery of his will."

A. The Practical Content of Revelation

God has filled us in on great spiritual truths concerning life, death, God, man, and eternity. He also has given us prudence, which is practical wisdom concerning earthly things such as solving problems.

We are under the authority of the Word of God, which calls us to obey. Paul said, "Let the word of Christ dwell in you richly" (Col. 3:16). Christians are called to submit to the Word of God—we don't chart our own course. When we meet together to plan, pray, and serve the Lord, one thing is central in our minds: What does the Word of God say about this matter? That should be the focus of everything we do.

B. The Personal Commitment to Revelation

On one particular occasion I was unable to attend a pastors' luncheon I had been invited to. Someone made the comment that I didn't go because I couldn't find a biblical route to get there. I took that as a compliment!

The church I pastor has the same kind of reputation for having a biblical perspective. It also is thoroughly committed to the Word of God. My commitment to Scripture led me to seminary because although I knew what the Bible said, I didn't know what it meant. In seminary I learned to understand the Bible. That prepared me to teach the Bible, which is a great joy for me.

Having a Mind to Submit to God's Word

When I came to Grace church following the untimely death of their pastor, my candidating sermon was an exposition of Romans 7. Because I had a tremendous burden to explain that difficult chapter and was oblivious to all else, I spoke for one hour and thirty-five minutes. Afterwards, some of the people came up and said, "That's what we want—but could you shorten it a little bit?" I thought, *If I get to preach here more than once, I can shorten it up all you want!*

One of the elders said, "We are ready to serve. We want to know what God wants us to do." That has been the commitment of Grace church throughout its history. I discovered in those first few days that the people had a mind to submit to God's Word. Since that time, the motto of the church has been "[equipping] the saints for the work of the ministry" (Eph. 4:12).

Christians mature by studying and applying Scripture: "All scripture is given by inspiration of God . . . that the man of God may be perfect, thoroughly furnished unto all good works" (2 Tim. 3:16-17). Church leaders are to equip people with "the sword of the Spirit, which is the word of God" (Eph. 6:17). More than merely owning a Bible, we're to understand the Bible so that we can use it effectively (cf. vv. 10-12).

A minister attending a pastors' conference told me, "If I told my people to do what you have told yours to do, they'd throw me out of the church." I said, "But it's biblical." He said, "It wouldn't matter to them." His church doesn't have a right perspective on the authority of God's Word. A church must be committed to biblical teaching and willing to serve under its authority.

VI. CALLED WITH: Unification (v. 10)

"That in the dispensation of the fullness of times he might gather together in one all things in Christ."

God's ultimate purpose is to gather all things together in Christ at the completion of redemptive history. The church is the symbol of that gathering now. We are called to be one in the family of God. When I was growing up, spiritual isolation was common. Everyone kept his spirituality to himself. It was something you didn't talk about. You smiled the Christian smile, carried the zipper Bible, and went to Sunday school. People didn't let anything out or anyone into their inner selves. Fellowship for most Christians was little more than red punch and stale cookies. There was little depth to it. But we have been called into a marvelous fellowship of unity.

In Philippians 2:2 Paul says that Christians should be "of the same mind, maintaining the same love, united in spirit, intent on one purpose" (NASB). Our love for others must be based on humility. That's why Paul said, "Look not every man on his own things, but every man also on the things of others" (v. 4), which was beautifully exemplified by Christ, who humbled Himself (vv. 5-8). To have unity, we must love one another with a spirit of humility. As long as everyone is looking out for himself, there can be no give-and-take relationship. When we recognize the reality of sin in our lives, we will realize how needy we are. Genuine humility is the result. That's why I don't preach the "self-help gospel," which says, "You're all right; think positive; be somebody." Show

106

me a church where that kind of message is preached, and I'll show you a church that doesn't know the meaning of fellowship. Everyone is there for himself—not for the benefit of anyone else. On the other hand, show me a church where the message of humility is taught, and I'll show you a church where people can love each other.

Love born of genuine humility is not the result of people trying to improve their self-image. Rather, it comes from giving to others who have needs. A church is a group of people called to interact with each other. Christians are not spectators. They are accountable to minister to others in love. They are committed to teaching others to minister because ministry to others is a goal of the church.

VII. CALLED UNTO: Glorification (v. 11)

"In whom also we have obtained an inheritance."

Peter described our inheritance as being that which is "incorruptible, and undefiled, and that fadeth not away, reserved in heaven for you" (1 Pet. 1:4). Christians are committed to glorification. Our focus is future. We are not citizens of this world. Philippians 3:20 says, "Our citizenship is in heaven." We're not earthbound, tied to the evil world's system. We have been made heirs of a boundless, eternal inheritance. That's why I don't preach purely political or social messages, for those have only temporal relevance. Christians belong to the kingdom of God, which is cutting its path by the power of the Spirit through the world of darkness. We look for a coming kingdom of glory.

Colossians 3:1-2 says, "If ye, then, be risen with Christ, seek those things which are above. . . . Set your affection on things above, not on things on the earth." We look for Jesus to return and His kingdom to be fully established. Consequently, we're not investing our lives and all our assets in this passing world. A church can have effective ministries only when people give generously instead of hoarding their resources to waste them on this world (1 John 2:17). They await the fullness of God's kingdom and a glorious eternal inheritance. In the words of Hebrews 11, we look "for a city . . . whose builder and maker is God" (v. 10).

VIII. CALLED FOR: Proclamation (v. 6)

"To the praise of the glory of his grace."

We have been called to proclaim the glory of God's grace. The world should look at us and say, "Look at that group of people! What a gracious God they have!" God should be glorified in the way we live and in the words we say. There's a sense in which we proclaim God's glory to Him and to His holy angels, as well as to the world around us. We have been redeemed to praise His glory. Consequently, the world cannot understand us unless it understands the glory of God, for we are its primary manifestation.

The glory of God is the greatest theme in the Bible and our most important checkpoint in life. Ask yourself this one question when you come to a crossroad: *Will my decision glorify God?* The church was established to be the praise of His glory. Our Lord put it this way: "Let your light so shine before men, that they may see your good works, and glorify your Father, who is in heaven" (Matt. 5:16).

Focusing on the Facts

1. Define the meaning of the word *church* as determined by its Greek counterpart in the New Testament (see p. 96).
2. Explain how the true church has always been led (see p. 97).
3. What is the main goal of the church in relation to the kingdom (see p. 97)?
4. When were the people who believe in Christ chosen by God (Eph. 1:4; see p. 98)?
5. What have redeemed people been called out of? What have they been transferred into (Col. 1:13; see p. 99)?
6. For what purpose have Christians been called from the world (see p. 102)?
7. What must a church emphasize so its people might live in reverential fear of God (see p. 102)?
8. With whom are Christians intimately identified? Support your answer with Scripture (see pp. 103-4).
9. What has God filled us with and given us (Eph. 1:8; see p. 104)?
10. When Christians meet together to plan, pray, and serve the Lord, what should be their central concern (see p. 105)?

11. How do Christians mature (see pp. 105-6)?
12. How can a church experience unity? What happens in a church where a self-help message is preached? Why (see pp. 106-7)?
13. What have Christians been called to proclaim (see p. 108)?

Pondering the Principles

1. Colossians 1:13-14 tells that the Father has "delivered us from the domain of darkness, and transferred us to the kingdom of His beloved Son, in whom we have redemption, the forgiveness of sins" (NASB). That act of mercy is something we will be eternally grateful for. Thank God for having graciously redeemed you from the "domain of darkness" and granted you entrance into "the kingdom of His beloved Son."

2. Meditate on Luke 6:46-49. When you find that the Bible says you should be doing something that you aren't, or that you shouldn't be doing something that you are, do you immediately attempt to make the necessary changes in your life? Or, do you procrastinate until the action you need to take no longer seems important to you? Commit yourself to applying biblical principles to your daily life so that you will have a solid foundation. What is the foundation of your life—Christ or this passing world (1 John 2:17)?

3. The Christian message is one of hope. Jesus is coming to usher His people into the glory of His kingdom. Knowing that, as well as the fact that He has saved us from sin and empowered us to live for Him, be sure to seek "the things above, where Christ is, seated at the right hand of God" (Col. 3:1, NASB). Is the majority of your time and energy put into things that have relatively little lasting significance, or do you spend your time on things that have eternal value? Are you a law-abiding citizen of heaven? Meditate on Philippians 3:17–4:1. Are you following a godly example so that you might become a more loyal citizen (v. 17)? Are you eagerly awaiting our Savior (v. 20)? How should your hope in Christ affect your life now (4:1)?

7

Doing the Lord's Work in the Lord's Way—Part 1

Outline

Introduction
A. The Lord's Work Identified
B. The Lord's Work Described
   1. It is demanding
   2. It is exhausting
   3. It is rewarding
      a) The alternative
      b) The analogy
   4. It is exciting
I. A Vision for the Future (v. 5)
A. The Pattern
B. The Preparation
   1. Exemplified
      a) In the life of Nehemiah
      b) In the life of William Carey
   2. Exhorted
II. A Sense of Flexibility (vv. 6-7)
A. Exemplified in the Life of Paul
B. Exemplified in the Life of David Livingstone
III. A Commitment to Thoroughness (vv. 6-7)
A. Exhorted
B. Experienced
C. Exemplified
   1. By Paul
   2. By Jesus
IV. A Commitment to Present Service (vv. 8-9)
A. Explained

Conclusion

Some Scriptures don't appear to have much spiritual value at first glance. But a thorough study can often uncover valuable insights. Much of 1 Corinthians 16 is that way:

"Now I will come unto you, when I shall pass through Macedonia; for I do pass through Macedonia. And it may be that I will abide, yea, and winter with you, that ye may bring me on my journey wherever I go. For I will not see you now by the way; but I trust to tarry a while with you, if the Lord permit. But I will tarry at Ephesus until Pentecost. For a great door, and effectual, is opened unto me, and there are many adversaries. Now if Timothy come, see that he may be with you without fear; for he worketh the work of the Lord, as I also do. Let no man, therefore, despise him, but conduct him forth in peace, that he may come unto me; for I look for him with the brethren. As touching our brother Apollos, I greatly desired him to come unto you with the brethren, but his will was not at all to come at this time; but he will come when he shall have a convenient time" (vv. 5-12).

A. The Lord's Work Identified

It sounds as if Paul was being ambivalent: "I'm going here; I might go there. If Timothy arrives, take care of him. I wanted Apollos to come, but he didn't want to." You might wonder how anyone could benefit from such seemingly insignificant material. The key to the text is the phrase "the work of the Lord." It first appears in verse 58 of chapter 15: "Therefore, my beloved brethren, be ye steadfast, unmovable, always abounding in the work of the Lord." Verse 10 of chapter 16 says, "If Timothy come, see that he may be with you without fear; for he worketh the work of the Lord, as I also do." That helps reveal what Paul is talking about in the verses in between—the work of the Lord. He was saying, "You ought to be always abounding in the work of the Lord, as Timothy and I are."

B. The Lord's Work Described

1. It is demanding

Those who do the Lord's work ought to be "unmovable, always abounding" in it. We ought to be overdoing it! When someone comes up to you and says, "You're doing too much," perhaps you are properly applying 1 Corinthians 15:58. Doing the work of the Lord is a vital responsibility.

What Is the Lord's Work?

To answer that question, you have to find out what work the Lord did when He was on earth. He basically did two things: He evangelized and He edified. Luke 19:10 says, "The Son of man is come to seek and to save that which was lost." That's evangelism. Acts 1:2-3 says, "Until the day in which [Jesus] was taken up [into heaven, He was] . . . speaking of the things pertaining to the kingdom of God." That refers to the edification of Christ's disciples. Jesus preached the gospel to people who didn't know Him and taught the people who did. Jesus spent a significant part of His ministry proclaiming the gospel to the masses. After He finished doing that, He often would teach His disciples to increase their faith.

2. It is exhausting

The Bible never describes the work of the Lord as being easy. "Work" and "labor" in verse 58 carry the idea of working to the point of exhaustion. Commentator G. Campbell Morgan said that Paul had in mind the "kind of toil that has in it the red blood of sacrifice, that kind of toil that wears and weakens by the way" (*The Corinthian Letters of Paul* [Old Tappan, N.J.: Revell, 1946], p. 207). Paul said this about Epaphroditus: "For the work of Christ, he was near unto death" (Phil. 2:30). That young man nearly worked himself to death. He is a good example of someone who was always abounding in the work of the Lord.

3. It is rewarding

"Your labor is not in vain" when you abound in the Lord's work (v. 58). It won't be empty, pointless, useless, or unproductive. Rather it will make a difference and produce fruit.

a) The alternative

Many people are busy in the church, but I'm not sure they are all doing the Lord's work of evangelism and edification. In Christianity, there is often busyness without fruitfulness. The lack of fruit may be attributed to laziness or to unwillingness to evangelize and edify others. However, God wants us to work hard in serving Him.

b) The analogy

The construction of a building has three phases that are analogous to doing the work of the Lord. A building first has to be planned by an architect, then it must be constructed according to the city's building code, and then it has to pass the inspection of an engineer who evaluates the quality of the workmanship. Similarly, when you do the work of the Lord, you have to follow the plan the Spirit of God lays out and adhere to the code of service that God has established in Scripture. The divine Inspector will tell you if your work has any lasting value.

We need to do the Lord's work according to His plans in order to receive His seal of approval. That's why 2 Timothy 2:15 says, "Be diligent to present yourself approved to God as a workman who does not need to be ashamed" (NASB). When the Inspector checks my work, I don't want to be ashamed.

Work hard and meet the standards so that He will approve your work. Don't build with "wood, hay, stubble," or other inexpensive or volatile materials;

114

rather build with "gold, silver, [and] precious stones" (1 Cor. 3:12). Then your works of service will last when they are tested at "the judgment seat of Christ" (2 Cor. 5:10). At that time the Lord will decide which works were good and which were worthless. There are Christians who will stand that day with the Lord, but their works will be destroyed by Christ's judgment fire. They constituted activity without productivity.

4. It is exciting

Christians have been called to do the Lord's work the Lord's way, and that ought to thrill us. Do you realize that the Almighty God, the Ruler of heaven and earth has said, "Would you be My personal envoys, taking My message to people around the world for as long as you live?" William Barclay has correctly said, "It is not the man who glorifies the work but the work which glorifies the man. There is no dignity like the dignity of a great task" (*The Letters to the Corinthians* [Philadelphia: Westminster, 1975], p. 165).

Lesson

Paul, describing his work and that of Timothy and Apollos, gives us seven practical principles for doing the Lord's work as He wants it done.

I. A VISION FOR THE FUTURE (v. 5)

Anyone committed to the Lord's work and motivated to reach others is going to see many needs that haven't been met yet. Therefore he will always be planning how to meet them. Such a person has a visionary perspective. He is never satisfied with what is being done. He focuses on what is not being done and that is why he plans ahead, looking for new worlds to conquer. He faces the reality of unmet opportunity, waiting for new doors to open.

A. The Pattern

1. Stated

In 1 Corinthians 16:5 Paul says, "I will come unto you, when I shall pass through Macedonia; for I do pass through Macedonia." Apparently Paul wrote 1 Corinthians at the end of a three-year stay in the city of Ephesus. Timothy delivered the letter. According to 2 Corinthians 1:15-16, Paul had originally planned to follow Timothy to Corinth, go to Macedonia, and then return to Corinth. Although he had a plan, he changed it, deciding first to head straight to Macedonia, then to Corinth, and finally to Jerusalem.

In 1 Corinthians 4:18-19 Paul says, "Now some are puffed up [conceited], as though I would not come to you. But I will come to you shortly, if the Lord will." Paul wanted to go to the Corinthian church because it was struggling with internal problems. So he decided to come and stay for the winter. Then they could give him some supplies so that he could continue on from there. Paul was planning ahead. He was busy in Ephesus—God was working through him, and many people were being saved and growing spiritually. But he also had a vision for what he needed to do in Corinth and Macedonia before returning to Jerusalem.

Anyone who does the Lord's work in the Lord's way must have a sense of vision. He must be able to analyze what isn't being done and strategize to get it done. He cannot have blinders on or focus only on immediate personal tasks. It has been said that Paul was always haunted by the regions beyond. He never saw a ship at anchor that he didn't wish to board so that he could spread the good news. He never saw a distant mountain range that he didn't want to cross so he could build up the saints. Paul had a vision for a world yet unreached. He could never be satisfied with what was happening where he was.

2. Supported

Romans 15 provides a glimpse of Paul's visionary strategizing: "Whenever I take my journey into Spain, I will come to you [the church at Rome]. . . . When, therefore, I have performed this, and have sealed to them this fruit, I will come by you into Spain" (vv. 24, 28). Paul had set his sights on Spain because no missionary had ever been there. Spain was in a blaze of glory at that time as part of the Roman Empire. Some of the greatest writers and orators were living in Spain. In fact the philosopher Seneca, who became the tutor of Nero and a prime minister of the Roman Empire, was a very influential man in Spain. No doubt Paul was excited about the impact that the gospel would have on such a place.

Paul was able to give himself fully to a task and yet still maintain a vision for the future. You cannot get bogged down with your present demands to the point that you assume there is nothing else left to do. One of the challenges of the ministry is the fact that you never finish the work. No matter what you do, there is always something that isn't being done.

B. The Preparation

1. Exemplified

It is important to prepare for the opportunities God gives you. Many people realize there is much to do in the future. But often they do nothing to get ready.

a) In the life of Nehemiah

Nehemiah didn't approach King Artaxerxes and say, "I would like a ministry. Could you please find something for me to do with my people?" Rather he said, "My people have a problem: they need their city and its wall rebuilt. I want to do it and have already figured out how it can be done. I'm just waiting for your permission." The king then allowed Nehemiah to accomplish his plans.

If you have a vision for the future, you need to strategize in the present to make the future a reality whenever God presents the opportunity. The reason some people never enter a particular ministry they are waiting for is that they have not planned for it or proved themselves worthy of doing it. We have to work to prove ourselves useful in the present so that we will be ready when the opportunity is presented.

b) In the life of William Carey

William Carey, the great pioneer of modern missions, made and repaired shoes in England. While he worked at his trade, he wept and prayed over a map of the world that he kept before him in his shop. After years of studying and strategizing, God sent him to work in India. He opened up that nation to the gospel for every missionary who has gone there since. God used a man with a vision for the future who was faithful in the present and proved himself capable.

2. Exhorted

Some in seminary are merely going through the motions of getting a degree. Because they are not involved in an effective, dynamic ministry in the present, they are not proving themselves faithful for a future ministry. People like that are not strategizing for the future. When they graduate, they will not have anything to do because they have not prepared themselves. They have failed to evaluate the church's need and to establish a strategy.

When God wants someone to perform a ministry, He chooses the person who is ready to do it—someone who has a plan and has proved himself faithful. While I was preaching across the country for Talbot Theological Seminary, I was planning how I would pastor a church when God gave me the opportunity. By the time the Lord opened the door for me to pastor Grace church, I had a good idea of how I would begin my ministry. I was framing my philosophy of ministry during my years on the preaching circuit. Once the door opened, I was ready.

What are you planning to do? Where is your vision? There is a whole world without God. What is your strategy to reach someone for Christ? To develop your spiritual gifts? To use your ministry to its fullest potential? If you aimlessly float from day to day, saying, "I'm just waiting for God to give me something to do," you'll never be given anything. However, if you're doing the Lord's work in the Lord's way, you will have a vision for the future.

II. A SENSE OF FLEXIBILITY (vv. 6-7)

The future may not come together as you think it will, so you have to be flexible. Some people think they know exactly what God wants them to do, and until something happens that exactly fits their list of expectations, they don't do anything. That's poor reasoning in following God's will. When you convince yourself that you can determine your future, you eliminate an important element of Christian service. Doing the Lord's work in the Lord's way demands a sense of flexibility.

A. Exemplified in the Life of Paul

In 1 Corinthians 16:6-7 Paul says, "It may be that I will abide, yea, and winter with you, that ye may bring me on my journey wherever I go. For I will not see you now by the way; but I trust to tarry a while with you, if the Lord permit." Paul had the unsettled attitude of an adventurer. He had wonderful plans, but he remained flexible and acknowledged that God had the right to change them midstream.

1. 2 Corinthians 1:15-17—The Corinthians accused Paul of being fickle. Paul responded, "I was minded to come unto you before . . . and to pass by you into Macedonia, and to come again out of Macedonia unto you, and of you to be brought on my way to Judea. When I, therefore, was thus minded, did I use lightness? Or the

things that I purpose, do I purpose according to the flesh, that with me there should be yea, yea, and nay, nay?" Paul did the best he could under the circumstances. That's all any of us can do.

That's the adventure of the ministry. Sometimes I may say, "We ought to do this, and we're going to do that." Then, three months later, I might say, "We've decided that we're not going to do that after all because it doesn't seem to be the Lord's will." That's in line with Paul's teaching, who qualified his plans by saying, "If the Lord permit" (1 Cor. 16:7).

2. Acts 16:6-10—Paul had learned a great lesson early in his ministry. He had been to Phrygia and Galatia and was planning to go through the major cities of Asia Minor: Ephesus, Laodicea, Pergamum, Smyrna, Thyatira, Sardis, and Philadelphia. I'm sure he had his strategy all mapped out. However, look what happened: "When they had gone throughout Phrygia and the region of Galatia, [they] were forbidden by the Holy Spirit to preach the word in Asia" (v. 6). Paul and his companions decided, "If we can't go south, we must go north. Let's go to Bithynia." But verse 7 says that "the Spirit allowed them not." Their only option was to go west.

For three hundred miles they walked west. They didn't know where they were going, but they knew that was the only place to go. They knew an open door was ahead somewhere.

When they came to Troas, "a vision appeared to Paul in the night: there stood a man of Macedonia, beseeching him, and saying, Come over into Macedonia and help us. And after he had seen the vision, immediately we endeavored to go into Macedonia, assuredly gathering that the Lord had called us to preach the gospel unto them" (vv. 9-10). What flexibility! They had their plans, and even though they were scuttled, they kept on moving. If you've ever tried to steer a car that's standing still, you know it is very difficult. But once it gets rolling, it's much easier to maneuver.

B. Exemplified in the Life of David Livingstone

Did you know that David Livingstone, the world-re-
nowned explorer and missionary to Africa, had originally
set his heart on going to China? He was disappointed he
didn't get there until he realized that God's will was for
him to go elsewhere. Livingstone ended up doing for Africa what Carey did for India: he opened it up to the mission-
aries who would follow.

III. A COMMITMENT TO THOROUGHNESS (vv. 6-7)

The work of the Lord must not be done superficially. In verse 6
Paul says, "It may be that I will abide, yea, and winter with
you." Paul apparently did spend the winter with the Corinthians. He probably wrote his first letter to them in the spring
from Ephesus, where he stayed until June. Then he went on to
be with the Corinthians and spent the winter months there. In
verse 7 Paul says, "I trust to tarry a while with you." Paul had
a commitment to thoroughness in the ministry. When he saw
the need of the Corinthians, he realized the only thing he
could do was commit himself to them long-term.

A. Exhorted

That commitment to thoroughness reflects the commission
our Lord gave in Matthew 28:19-20: "Go therefore and
make disciples of all the nations . . . teaching them to ob-
serve all that I commanded you" (NASB). You cannot
teach someone to follow everything God has commanded
without investing your life in that person. Discipline cannot be superficial. It takes time.

Paul had no intention of making a quick stop in Corinth.
He knew the needs were great, as evidenced by the con-
tents of 1 Corinthians. He had spent eighteen months
there the first time and now wanted to spend at least another winter there. He spent three years ministering in
Ephesus. He went to Galatia on his first, second, and third
missionary journeys because he wanted to accomplish a
thorough work there.

B. Experienced

I'm in the pastorate because that is where I believe I can do the most thorough work. When I traveled on the preaching circuit for two-and-a-half years before coming to Grace, I spoke thirty-five to forty times a month. I'd present a church with biblical truth for one to four days and then leave town and go on to another church. That frustrated me because my messages were usually in the context of evangelistic meetings and were limited to topics such as prophecy, the Holy Spirit, and worldliness. I felt as if I wasn't doing anything with depth. Then Grace church came into my life. The Lord fulfilled the desire of my heart to do something that did not seem as superficial.

C. Exemplified

1. By Paul

   a) Colossians 1:27-28—God made "known what is the riches of the glory of this mystery among the Gentiles, which is Christ in you, the hope of glory; whom we preach, warning every man, and teaching every man in all wisdom, that we may present every man perfect in Christ Jesus." Paul wanted to teach everything to everyone all the time so that they could become mature in the faith. That's a commitment to thoroughness!

   b) 1 Thessalonians 3:10—Paul was with the Thessalonians for only three Sabbaths. Although circumstances made it necessary for him to leave soon, he had a great desire to minister to them in a thorough way. He told them of his eagerness to see them again— and that he and his companions were praying "night and day" that they "might perfect that which [was] lacking in [their] faith." Since Paul had stayed in Thessalonica for only a few weeks, he spent day and night agonizing in prayer that God might allow him to go back and build up the Thessalonian saints to maturity.

   c) Ephesians 4:11-13—The Lord has given the church evangelists and pastors to bring it to "the measure of the stature of the fullness of Christ" (v. 13). His goal is to build the saints to maturity. Paul recognized that, for he told the Ephesians, "I have not shunned to declare unto you all the counsel of God" (Acts 20:27). He thoroughly instructed the believers. He wanted them to understand everything that would help them mature.

2. By Jesus

In praying to the Father in John 17, Jesus reports that He has done the work that the Father has given Him to do (vv. 4, 8). Jesus had faithfully given the Father's Word to the disciples. He was thorough—His training of the Twelve took Him three years.

As we prepare to serve Christ as His ambassadors, we must do so with a commitment to excellence. We ought to be doing it to the limit of our capacity. Then our labor will not be in vain.

IV. A COMMITMENT TO PRESENT SERVICE (vv. 8-9)

A. Explained

There are plenty of dreamers who are planning what they will do, but far fewer doers who are *doing* what they should do. Young men in seminary often have great expectations about the ministry they want to be part of. But what are they doing in the present? The present is the proving ground for the future. I'll never forget talking to a seminary student who was graduating in one month. He said, "I have finished four years of seminary and have a great deal of information in my head. I'm going to be pastoring a church, but I don't have any idea what's required of me!" If you think that was bad for him, imagine the poor folks he was going to be ministering to! A seminarian cannot expect to suddenly become a man with all the answers. He has to be a proved commodity.

We constantly receive letters from churches and organizations wanting us to recommend people for ministry. They almost always request someone who has proved to be effective. I can't say I blame them. In fact, God is the same way. I don't believe a novice should be given a strategic place of ministry. Anyone without experience who is planning for the future must commit himself to prepare in the present. Sometimes it is hard to keep a balance between the two, but diligence and faithfulness in the present are necessary for a smooth transition into areas of greater responsibility in the future.

Paul understood the tension that existed between his visionary plans and his present ministry. He told the Corinthians about his plans to pass through Macedonia and visit them. But first he had to finish what he was doing in Ephesus: "I will tarry at Ephesus until Pentecost. For a great door, and effectual, is opened unto me" (vv. 8-9). He had a ministry he couldn't neglect. His great plans for other churches had to be deferred until Pentecost.

Conclusion

If you are going to do the Lord's work the Lord's way, you will need to have a vision for the future, a sense of flexibility, a commitment to thoroughness, and a commitment to your present ministry. When the time comes for God to send you to another area, you will have been prepared and approved. Whatever your gifts and callings are, always be abounding in the work of the Lord so that your work is not in vain but to His glory.

Focusing on the Facts

1. What two things constitute the work of the Lord? Explain how Jesus accomplished both (see p. 113).
2. What characteristic of the Lord's work did Epaphroditus demonstrate (see p. 113)?
3. Explain how Christians can be busy without being fruitful (see p. 114).
4. How is doing the Lord's work like the process of constructing a building (see p. 114)?
5. When will the value of every Christian's work be tested? Will some Christians have their works destroyed? Explain (see pp. 114-15).

6. On what will the Christian with a vision for the future focus (see p. 115)?
7. What were Paul's plans for visiting the Corinthian church (1 Cor. 16:5; see p. 116)?
8. While Paul was in Corinth, where was he planning to go (Rom. 15:24, 28; see p. 117)?
9. How did Nehemiah and William Carey prepare for doors that the Lord later opened (see pp. 117-18)?
10. What is one reason some people never enter the ministry they are anticipating (see p. 118)?
11. When God wants someone to perform a ministry, whom does He most likely choose (see p. 118)?
12. Although Paul had established plans, what did he know God had the right to do (see p. 119)?
13. Explain how Paul and his companions had their plans changed while trying to minister in Asia Minor (see p. 120).
14. Explain how the Great Commission demands a commitment to thoroughness (Matt. 28:19-20; see p. 121).
15. Why did Paul spend day and night agonizing in prayer over the Thessalonians (see p. 122)?
16. Why did Paul "declare . . . all the counsel of God" (Acts 20:27; see p. 123)?
17. Explain how Jesus finished the work that the Father gave Him to do (John 17:4, 8; see p. 123).
18. What must you be doing if you want God to use you in the future? Why (see p. 123)?
19. What is necessary for a smooth transition into areas of greater responsibility (see pp. 123-24)?

Pondering the Principles

1. How are you involved in the Lord's work of evangelism and edification? Are you sharing the gospel and your testimony with your relatives, friends, and neighbors? Are you discipling another Christian, teaching a class, or participating in some other ministry that is enabling Christians to grow? Consider what a great privilege it is to serve God Almighty.

2. What are your plans for ministering to others in the next month? in the next year? in five years? in ten years? You may not be on the church staff, but you should still have a vision for the fu-

ture. Do you recognize any needs you are prepared to meet now? Is the Lord bringing to your attention any needs that you would have to prepare yourself to meet? Prayerfully strategize how you will accomplish those goals, even if they seem to be beyond your ability right now.

3. Are your plans flexible? Do you acknowledge that God has the right to change them midstream? Meditate on James 4:13-17. Do you qualify your plans with, "If the Lord wills" (v. 15, NASB)? Planning without consulting the Lord is a prideful act of self-sufficiency. According to verse 17 what is the opposite extreme of not doing anything at all? Memorize Proverbs 3:5-6.

4. Like many, you may find it easy to start out well but difficult to follow a task through to completion. We live in a society that expects instant results and is characterized by shallow, short-term commitments. Are you willing to commit yourself fully to whatever the Lord has directed you to do—no matter how long it takes? Follow the example of Paul, who pursued the Lord's work with such thoroughness that at the end of his life he could say, "I have fought the good fight, I have finished the course, I have kept the faith; in the future there is laid up for me the crown of righteousness, which the Lord, the righteous Judge, will award to me on that day" (2 Tim. 4:7-8, NASB).

8
Doing the Lord's Work in the Lord's Way—Part 2

Outline

Introduction
A. The Requirement of Working
B. The Reward of Working

Review
  I. A Vision for the Future (v. 5)
 II. A Sense of Flexibility (vv. 6-7)
III. A Commitment to Thoroughness (vv. 6-7)
 IV. A Commitment to Present Service (vv. 8-9)
      A. Explained

Lesson
      B. Exemplified
          1. The faithful servant
          2. The wise steward
          3. The Philadelphian church
          4. The apostle Paul
              a) The place of opportunity
              b) The pursuit of opportunity
                 (1) Recognized
                 (2) Reviewed
      C. Exhorted
  V. An Acceptance of Opposition as a Challenge (vv. 8-9)
      A. Exemplified by the Apostle Paul
          1. His reason
          2. His reflection
      B. Exemplified by John Paton

VI. A Team Spirit (vv. 10-11)
  A. A Lack of a Personal Agenda
  B. A Recognition of Fellow Christians
VII. A Sensitivity to the Spirit's Leading in Others (v. 12)

  Conclusion

Introduction

Did I Do My Best?

Keith L. Brooks tells a story in his *Illustrations for Preachers and Speakers* that is especially appropriate as we consider doing the Lord's work in the Lord's way ([Grand Rapids: Zondervan, 1946], pp. 75-76). Northwestern University, located in Evanston, Illinois, once had a volunteer lifesaving crew to rescue people from ships that were in distress on Lake Michigan. One time the *Lady Elgin*, a passenger ship, foundered offshore. A member of the crew who participated in the rescue attempt was a young student at Garrett Biblical Institute. His name was Edward W. Spencer, and he was preparing for a lifetime of missionary service. He saw a woman clinging to some wreckage far out in the breakers. So he dove in the water and swam out to bring her safely to shore. Seeing more victims in the water, Spencer swam out again and again until finally he had rescued seventeen people by himself. Then, collapsing in a delirium of exhaustion, he cried out, "Did I do my best? Did I do my best?" When his brother informed him of how many lives he had saved, Spencer replied, "If only I could have saved one more!" Did he do his best? I'd say he did!

  A. The Requirement of Working

    The only acceptable way to do the work of the Lord is by doing your best. First Corinthians 15:58 says, "Therefore, my beloved brethren, be ye steadfast, unmovable, always abounding in the work of the Lord, forasmuch as ye know that your labor is not in vain in the Lord." That deserves our very best. Every Christian should ask, "Did I do my best?"

1. 2 Timothy 2:15—"Be diligent to present yourself approved to God as a workman who does not need to be ashamed" (NASB).

2. Mark 13:32-33—Referring to His second coming the Lord said, "Of that day and that hour knoweth no man, no, not the angels who are in heaven, neither the Son, but the Father. Take heed, watch and pray; for ye know not when the time is." We don't know when the Lord is going to return. We don't know how much time we have before the resurrection of believers occurs and we are glorified. Then Jesus said, "The Son of man is like a man taking a far journey, who left his house and gave authority to his servants, and to every man his work, and commanded the porter to watch. Watch ye, therefore; for ye know not when the master of the house cometh" (vv. 34-35). One day soon He will come back and evaluate the quality of His servants' work.

3. Revelation 22:12—"Behold, I come quickly, and my reward is with me, to give every man according as his work shall be." How you do the work He has committed to you will determine how He will reward you in glory.

4. 1 Corinthians 15:50-58—Paul told the Corinthians that since they didn't know how much time they had before the Lord's return, they ought to be always doing the Lord's work. There's no time to waste!

5. 2 Thessalonians 3:11—Paul said, "We hear that there are some who walk among you disorderly, working not at all but are busybodies." The Greek text incorporates a play on words, literally saying, "Not busy workers, but busybodies." Some of the people in the Thessalonian church were not working. Rather, they were apparently speculating about the return of Christ, failing to accomplish anything meaningful in their daily lives. Evidently some had laid down the tools of their trade and were burdening others. Therefore Paul said, "Them that are such we command and exhort, by our Lord Jesus Christ, that with quietness they work, and eat their own bread. But ye, brethren, be not weary in

well-doing" (vv. 12-13). Paul didn't want those who were obedient to get discouraged because of those who weren't working. If you are giving everything you've got while others are not, yet they are receiving the same pay and benefits, it may be easy to become discouraged. Christians must not be busybodies who only talk but busy workers who get the work done.

6. 1 Timothy 5:9-10—Paul instructed the church to provide only for those widows who had proved themselves faithful: "Let not a widow be taken into the number under sixty years old, having been the wife of one man, well reported of for good works, if she hath brought up children, if she hath lodged strangers, if she hath washed the saint's feet, if she hath relieved the afflicted, if she hath diligently followed every good work."

7. Ephesians 4:11-12—The pastor is to equip "the saints for the work of the ministry." Every Christian has an obligation to do the work of the ministry.

8. Revelation 2:2—Christ said to the church at Ephesus, "I know thy works, and thy labor."

9. 2 Corinthians 5:10—Christians will be rewarded on the basis of the work they have done in the name of Christ. The Lord will determine whether it was good or useless—in the words of 1 Corinthians 3:12, whether it was valuable, like "gold, silver, [and] precious stones"; or relatively worthless, like "wood, hay, [and] stubble."

10. John 9:4—Jesus said, "I must work the works of him that sent me, while it is day; the night cometh, when no man can work." Now is the time to do the Lord's work, making sure we are doing our best.

11. Colossians 4:17—"Take heed to the ministry which thou hast received in the Lord, that thou fulfill it."

12. Ephesians 5:15-16—If you're going to do the Lord's work at maximum output, you have to make the best use of the time available to you.

13. 1 Peter 5:8—Peter said, "Be sober." That imperative means we must set our priorities.

B. The Reward of Working

If we have established our priorities, made efficient use of our time, and worked diligently, we'll be in the same company as Jesus, who said, "I have finished the work which thou gavest me to do" (John 17:4). Like Paul, may we be able to say, "I finished my course" (2 Tim. 4:7). We'll have a sense of accomplishment in finishing the Lord's work only when we've put forth our complete effort. In the future the Lord will reward us in glory. In the present He will probably give us more work to do because we have proved our faithfulness.

Centuries ago a victor at the Olympic games was asked, "Spartan, what will you gain by this victory?" The athlete replied, "I will have the honor of fighting in the front line in the ranks of my king." That's a good attitude. If you do your work well in a lesser setting, you may be placed in the center of action. In a spiritual context, if you are faithful to the Lord and prove yourself successful in your work, He will probably promote you to an area of greater responsibility. Along with increased responsibility will come the need for greater effort and the possibility of greater consequences. That is encouraging because the bigger the challenge is, the bigger the victory will be.

Review

In 1 Corinthians 16:5-12 the apostle Paul describes his plans. Having just exhorted the Corinthians to always abound in the Lord's work (15:58), he indirectly describes how he accomplished that himself. Implied in this section are seven principles for doing the Lord's work the Lord's way.

I. A VISION FOR THE FUTURE (v. 5; see pp. 115-19)

II. A SENSE OF FLEXIBILITY (vv. 6-7; see pp. 119-21)

III. A COMMITMENT TO THOROUGHNESS (vv. 6-7; see pp. 121-23)

IV. A COMMITMENT TO PRESENT SERVICE (vv. 8-9)

  A. Explained (see pp. 123-24)

Lesson

  B. Exemplified

    1. The faithful servant

      Our Lord gives the parable of the talents in Matthew 25. In verse 23 the master says to his faithful servant, "Well done, good and faithful servant; thou hast been faithful over a few things, I will make thee ruler over many things." Faithfulness at a current level of responsibility gives one the right to be used at a higher level in the future.

      Many people want to have immediate success in ministry without there being a proving ground—a place where they perfect their skills and their spiritual gifts. Someone who does the Lord's work in the Lord's way doesn't only plan for the future; he ministers in the present as well.

    2. The wise steward

      Luke 12:42 records a similar exhortation: "The Lord said, Who, then, is that faithful and wise steward, whom his lord shall make ruler over his household?" A steward who was faithful in handling the affairs of the house was given the privilege of ruling it. Before you can expect God to drop you into a great and exciting ministry that has much at stake, you will have to prove yourself faithful at the level at which He has placed you now.

132

Paul, who had great hopes of visiting the Corinthians, resolved to stay at Ephesus to pursue the opportunity of service there. He was totally committed to His current ministry until God shut the door. He was never discontent about his area of service. He never considered his current ministry a stepping-stone to a better one. He gave his whole life in ministry to the church where God had directed him. When God closed that door and opened another, he gave his whole life to that.

Are You Looking for an Open Door?

Paul reported to the church at Antioch that God "had opened the door of faith unto the Gentiles" (Acts 14:27). In 2 Corinthians 2:12 he says, "When I came to Troas to preach Christ's gospel . . . a door was opened unto me of the Lord." Paul asked the Colossians to pray "that God would open . . . a door of utterance, to speak the [gospel] of Christ" (4:3). The open door simply signifies an opportunity to preach the gospel. Wherever there was a door of opportunity, Paul was ready to go through it. That is how we ought to be.

Some people get so picky about which door they go through that they miss the opportunities God puts before them. They wait around for something wonderful to happen, but it never happens because they are never willing to go through a door that God opens for them. Seminary students often specify the exact type of ministry situation in which they want to work. Many naively expect to find a perfect church. (If they found one, that church wouldn't need them!) Meanwhile, there is an open door at a church with all kinds of problems, but they don't pursue it because it doesn't exactly fit their expectations. If a door is open now, you should seriously consider entering it rather than doing nothing.

3. The Philadelphian church

The Lord told the church at Philadelphia that He was the One who "openeth, and no man shutteth; and shutteth, and no man openeth. . . . I have set before thee an open door, and no man can shut it" (Rev. 3:7-8). That church was very different from the dead church at Laodicea, which the Lord addressed next. Perhaps one of the things that can turn a Philadelphia into a Laodicea is a refusal to go through open doors. Such refusal results in apathy, which our Lord condemned with these words: "Because thou art lukewarm, and neither cold nor hot, I will spew thee out of my mouth" (Rev. 3:16).

When God opens the door and directs you to enter through it, He will empower you to do what He wants you to accomplish. Don't be content to do nothing, waiting for the perfect situation. Find an open door and go through it. If you haven't proved yourself faithful in entering the doors that the Lord has already opened for you, don't expect Him to open others for which you are unprepared. Don't be so independent and inflexible that you can't enter a door God has opened.

4. The apostle Paul

 a) The place of opportunity

According to 1 Corinthians 16:8-9, God had opened the door at Ephesus in a wonderful way. Ephesus was the major city in Asia Minor, a large province of the Roman Empire that now makes up the modern nation of Turkey. Ephesus was the second major city east of Rome. (The first was Corinth.) Although it was three miles from the sea, it was located on the navigable Cayster River, making it a center of commerce. It boasted one of the Seven Wonders of the World: the temple of Diana, which, among other things, served as an international bank. It was the meeting place for the leaders of the confederacy of Ionian states. The city was also a haven for criminals. Cultic and superstitious practices proliferated. The geographic setting and the climate of Ephesus were beautiful. The commerce of the city helped it to flourish. It may have been John's model for the economic system of the end times (Rev. 18:12-13).

b) The pursuit of opportunity

    (1) Recognized

        It is no wonder that Paul said of such an incredible city: "A wide door for effective [Gk., *energēs*, "energetic, productive"] service has opened to me" (1 Cor. 16:9, NASB). Although the city was crawling with sorcerers, magicians, prostitutes, and false teachers of every sort, Paul considered the city to be a wide-open opportunity for the gospel. Perhaps we would have concluded that it wouldn't be a good place to go. But God opened the door, and Paul recognized that.

    (2) Reviewed

        The door in Ephesus hadn't always been open. Paul had planned to go to Ephesus for a long time. Acts 16 records that Paul and his companions were determined to go south into Asia Minor but were forbidden by the Holy Spirit to do so (v. 7). So they went west into Macedonia. Later Paul headed east and went to Ephesus for one day, hoping to return at a later time (Acts 18:18-21). Eventually God opened a door for him to do so, after first preparing the city through the ministry of Apollos, who preached the Word of God mightily (v. 28). Apparently Ephesus needed to be warmed up for Paul, whose approach might have been too strong. Yet Paul might not have been ready for the opposition he was going to face in Ephesus, so the Lord allowed him to be beaten and jailed in Philippi—perhaps to toughen him up. When the preparation was complete and the time was right, God brought Paul to Ephesus. Paul apparently reasoned that since God had so carefully brought him there, he would stay until his work was done.

C. Exhorted

Don't ignore an open door. Where God has opened a door, someone has to go through it. I'm concerned about people who claim they're going to get into a ministry but aren't doing anything at present. They are only dreamers with no proving ground to test and establish their future methods of ministry. One who does the Lord's work in the Lord's way has plans for the future, but he also has a great commitment to the present. He pours his life into the present because he knows that that may be all he has.

Acts 13:1-2 illustrates the importance of being involved in the present. The church at Antioch had five pastors. Verse 2 says that "as they ministered to the Lord, and fasted, the Holy Spirit said, Separate me Barnabas and Saul for the work unto which I have called them." Because they had proved themselves faithful in their present ministries, the Holy Spirit called Paul and Barnabas to the ministry He had planned for them.

V. AN ACCEPTANCE OF OPPOSITION AS A CHALLENGE (vv. 8-9)

If you find a place that doesn't have any problems, then you are not needed there. Accept opposition as a challenge. Paul said, "I will tarry at Ephesus until Pentecost. For a great door, and effectual, is opened unto me, and there are many adversaries." That might appear to us to be a good reason not to stay—but not to Paul! G. Campbell Morgan once said that if you have no opposition in the place you are serving, you're serving in the wrong place (*The Corinthian Letters of Paul* [Old Tappan, N.J.: Revell, 1946], p. 213).

A. Exemplified by the Apostle Paul

1. His reason

In effect Paul was saying, "I have to stay in Ephesus because I can't leave the troops alone; there's too much opposition here!" The city of Ephesus was rough. The temple of Diana was the center of organized idolatry characterized by sexual perversion involving priestesses who were prostitutes. In addition, there were certain Jewish exorcists who claimed to cast out demons (Acts 19:13-17). There was prejudice, superstition, racism, sexual vice, religious animosity, paganism, idolatry—virtually everything that exists in any city in the world today existed there. Most people would look for a place that was more tame, but Paul accepted it as a challenge.

He went into Ephesus and began to teach the Word of God every day for more than two years (Acts 19:8-10). It is likely that those who were saved there were the ones who founded the other churches of Asia Minor mentioned in Revelation 2-3. Those who had practiced magical arts now burned their books (Acts 19:19), and so many people stopped buying idols of the goddess Diana that the craftsmen who made them angrily stirred up a demonstration (vv. 23-41). The gospel made quite an impact on Ephesus.

Choosing the Church with a Challenge

Paul saw opposition as a tremendous challenge. When you look for a ministry, seek one that isn't already everything it ought to be and see if God can use you to His glory to change it. The people you will minister to are those who need you the most. Find a city where the gospel is not preached, a church where the Word of God is not taught or one that does not have a biblical leadership structure, and instruct them in the truth. Put yourself where God can use you. When there are many adversaries, that's when the troops need you the most.

2. His reflection

In 2 Corinthians 1 Paul looks back on the battle in Ephesus: "We should like you, our brothers, to know something of the trouble we went through in Asia. At that time we were completely overwhelmed, the burden was more than we could bear, in fact we told ourselves that this was the end. Yet we believe now that we had this sense of impending disaster so that we might learn to trust, not in ourselves, but in God who can raise the dead" (vv. 8-9, Phillips). When you get into a desperate situation like that, don't rely on yourself; turn to God. That's when His power begins to flow, and the enemies begin to drop one by one!

137

In 2 Corinthians 4:10 Paul says, "Every day we experience something of the death of Jesus, so that we may also show the power of the life of Jesus in these bodies of ours" (Phillips). They faced death every day and experienced Christ's power. That's the excitement and the adventure of the ministry—charging into battle and confronting opposition in the power of Christ. That's when God gives us the victory. Take up the challenge and find a difficult place to minister!

B. Exemplified by John Paton

John Paton accepted an immense challenge. While he was a student at a Bible college in London, God called him to go to the cannibal-infested New Hebrides islands in the South Pacific. Some of us might have said, "Lord, You've got the wrong guy! Are You sure my gifts are fit for that? And besides, I graduated—I can make it in the ministry. No sense in my being someone's lunch after all the effort I've put in. I know a Bible college dropout who will never make it in the ministry. Send him there; they'll eat him, and who will know? He'll go down in history as having died a hero!"

But John Paton didn't argue with God. A ship dropped him and his wife off, and they rowed ashore to an island inhabited by cannibals whose language they did not speak. And the Lord miraculously preserved them. Later, when the chief of the tribe in that area was converted to Christ, he asked John who the army was that surrounded his hut every night. God's holy angels had stood guard. After a short time, Paton's wife gave birth to a baby, and both she and the baby died in childbirth. He was forced to sleep on the graves to keep the cannibals from digging up the bodies and eating them. In spite of the great challenge, he decided to stay. The adversaries were many, but that was where God wanted him. (His exciting story is told by James Paton, his brother, in *John G. Paton: Missionary to the New Hebrides* [Edinburgh: Banner of Truth Trust], 1965 reprint.)

How do you face such opposition? Only by totally depending on God. Accept the challenge, and watch God's power bring about victories you never dreamed possible.

VI. A TEAM SPIRIT (vv. 10-11)

Paul was a team-oriented leader. He didn't try to be a lone superstar. He depended on other people. In 1 Corinthians 16:10 he says, "If Timothy comes, see that he may be with you without fear." According to 1 Corinthians 4:17, Paul was sending Timothy to Corinth, perhaps with this letter. He warned the proud and self-willed Corinthians not to intimidate Timothy, saying, "He worketh the work of the Lord, as I also do. Let no man, therefore, despise him, but conduct him forth in peace, that he may come unto me; for I look for him with the brethren" (16:10-11). Paul asked the Corinthians to respect his emissary, whom he hoped would bring back a good report. Even though Timothy was Paul's son in the faith (1 Tim. 1:2), Paul considered him an equal. He was quick to stand up for his fellow-worker. Even though Paul was a leader among leaders, he recognized that he was simply a co-worker in God's service. He had a great sense of teamwork.

A. A Lack of a Personal Agenda

Paul had no personal agenda. When he was a prisoner and a new generation of preachers was coming along that the churches were beginning to follow, he didn't try to regain his prior place of preeminence. Evidently some of them claimed that Paul was a prisoner because he had botched his ministry. Paul noted that some "preach Christ of contention, not sincerely, supposing to add affliction to my bonds. . . . Notwithstanding . . . Christ is preached; and in that I do rejoice, yea, and will rejoice" (Phil. 1:16, 18). Paul was thrilled to support others who were doing the Lord's work. If they didn't do it the Lord's way, he reprimanded them; but anyone who did was on his team.

B. A Recognition of Fellow Christians

In Romans 16:3-15 Paul mentions twenty-four individuals and two individual households. Among them were seven women who also helped him in the work of the Lord. You can never minister for God in isolation. You must realize that you are but one member of God's team.

When we see Paul doing the Lord's work, we always see him teamed with Silas, Barnabas, Luke, Aristarchus,

Mark, or Timothy. One who does the Lord's work the Lord's way realizes that he is just part of the fellowship and that it is his job to encourage and edify others. That's why Paul requested that the Corinthians be respectful toward Timothy. Epaphroditus "was near unto death" (Phil. 2:30), and Paul was grateful that he didn't die because he needed his fellow worker. When Paul was old, he requested Timothy to bring Mark, saying, "He is profitable to me for the ministry" (2 Tim. 4:11). Paul had a sense of teamwork.

In 2 Timothy 4:5 he says to Timothy, "Watch thou in all things, endure afflictions, do the work of an evangelist, make full proof of thy ministry." That was a dramatic moment in Timothy's life. Up to that time, Timothy had served Paul. But now it was time for Paul to send him off to do his own work. The proving ground for Timothy was his service to Paul.

God has called some to lead and others to serve. Sometimes those who serve will do so throughout their entire ministry. Other times they'll serve for a period of apprenticeship, and then the Lord will call them out to lead on their own. But that sense of teamwork must be retained. Maybe we are called to support someone else or to lead on our own. Whatever it is, Jesus said to "love one another. By this shall all men know that ye are my disciples" (John 13:34-35). When the world sees the team working together as a team, they witness the validity of our faith.

VII. A SENSITIVITY TO THE SPIRIT'S LEADING IN OTHERS (v. 12)

We should be sensitive to the Spirit's leading in others, as Paul was in the ministry of Apollos: "As touching our brother Apollos, I greatly desired him to come unto you with the brethren" (1 Cor. 16:12). Paul wanted Apollos to go along with Timothy to Corinth, apparently to straighten out the divisions that had developed regarding Paul and Apollos in the church (1 Cor. 1:11-12). Although Paul was the greatest leader among the Gentile churches, he didn't force his authority upon Apollos. Verse 12 says, "His will was not at all to come at this time; but he will come when he shall have a convenient time."

You can't force people to do the Lord's work as you interpret it. You have to wait until the Spirit of God works in their hearts. Paul had authority, great ideas, and effective strategies; but he also had patience for God's Spirit to work in the hearts of the others on the team. He trusted their judgment. It is important to have a sense of teamwork and to realize that God's Spirit works in every Christian, not just in the leader. An effective leader has to be sensitive to what God is saying to other members on the team. Do not dominate the team. Rather, patiently let the Spirit of God generate ministries among the rest.

Conclusion

How does one do the Lord's work in the Lord's way? By having a vision for the future, flexibility, thoroughness, a commitment to the present, an acceptance of opposition, a team spirit, and sensitivity to the Holy Spirit's leading in the lives of others.

An English clergyman of the last century was asked how he accounted for the great success that the Methodist revival was having in England. He replied, "The answer is simple. They are all at it and they are always at it." I admire the dedication of those early Methodists. May we, too, be "always abounding in the work of the Lord, forasmuch as ye know that your labor is not in vain in the Lord" (1 Cor. 15:58).

Focusing on the Facts

1. What will determine how Christians will be rewarded in heaven (2 Cor. 5:10; Rev. 22:12; see pp. 129-30)?
2. Explain why Paul had to exhort those who were not working in the Thessalonian church (2 Thess. 3:11-13; see pp. 129-30).
3. What is the pastor's job (Eph. 4:11-12)? What is every Christian's obligation (see p. 130)?
4. How can we have a sense of accomplishment with regard to the Lord's work (see p. 131)?
5. When might the Lord promote us to an area of greater responsibility? What will accompany that (see p. 132)?

6. How were the faithful servant and wise steward rewarded (Matt. 25:23; Luke 12:42; see p. 132)?

7. Explain how Paul's attitude toward ministry motivated him to stay at Ephesus rather than go to Corinth as he had planned (see p. 133).

8. When God opens a door, what can we expect Him to do (see p. 134)?

9. How did God apparently prepare both Paul and Ephesus for his ministry there (see p. 135)?

10. When did God call Saul and Barnabas into another ministry (Acts 13:1-2; see p. 136)?

11. What effect did the gospel have on Ephesus and the surrounding area (see p. 137)?

12. What had Paul learned from the opposition he encountered at Ephesus (2 Cor. 1:8-9; see p. 137)?

13. Although Timothy was Paul's son in the faith, how did Paul view him (see p. 139)?

14. How did Paul demonstrate his lack of a personal agenda when another generation of preachers was arising while he was in prison (Phil. 1:16, 18; see p. 139)?

15. Describe some ways that Paul demonstrated a team spirit (see pp. 139-40).

16. How was Paul sensitive to the Spirit's leading of Apollos? Explain how we can be sensitive to the Spirit's leading of others (see pp. 140-41).

Pondering the Principles

1. Are you looking for an open door to serve others? Are you hoping only for a ministry opportunity in an upper middle-class suburb with a wonderful climate? Or, would you be willing to work in a city like Ephesus with all of its problems? Make sure your motive for serving the Lord is honorable. What are you currently doing to prepare for the open door you are looking for? Prove yourself faithful in entering the doors He opens for you, realizing that as He guides you through prayer, godly counsel, and circumstances, He will also empower you to do what He wants you to accomplish (1 Thess. 5:24).

2. Do you work well with fellow Christians? Do you prefer to do everything by yourself, or do you share your responsibilities with others? Delegation is a vital part of effective discipleship.

When you are ministering to others, include some fellow Christians on your team. Allow them to have firsthand experience. Then, when they are fully trained, be willing to let them begin their own ministries. If you are not gifted as a leader, but see yourself serving in a behind-the-scenes capacity, realize that you are still are an important part of the team. Whether you lead or serve, make sure that you minister "heartily, as to the Lord." Memorize Colossians 3:23-24.

Scripture Index

147

3:14-15	49
3:16	65
3:16-17	106
4:1-2	50
4:6-7	50
4:12	69
4:13	51
4:15	51
4:16	51
5:8	67
5:9-10	130
5:17	53
5:20	12, 54
6:1-2	68
6:11-12	12

2 Timothy

1:9	97-98
1:13-14	51-52
2:1-2	52
2:2	14
2:15	52, 114, 129
2:17-18	54
2:24-25	52
3:14-17	52
4:1-2	52-53
4:5	140
4:7	131
4:7-8	126
4:11	140

Titus

1:5	55
1:5-9	10, 62
1:7	11
1:8	11-12
1:9-11	54
1:13	26
2:2	68
2:3-5	14, 71
2:6-8	14, 69
2:9-10	68

Hebrews

10:24-25	25
10:25	26
11:10	107
12:23	44
13:17	66-67, 73

James

1:27	14, 102
4:13-17	126
5:16	26

1 Peter

1:16	102
2:2	63
5:1-4	64
5:2-4	55
5:4	66
5:8	131
5:10	97

2 Peter

1:4	80
3:3-4	87

1 John

1:3	103
2:15	102
2:15-17	99
2:17	107

Revelation

1:5	44
2:2	130
2:4	88
2:14	81
2:16	81
3:1	100
3:7-8	134
3:16	134
4:10	64, 87
17:1	45
18:12-13	134
22:12	87, 129

Topical Index

Olympic contender, attitude of
   one, 131
"One anothers." *See* Love
Open door. *See* Opportunity
Opportunity, looking for, 133-
   36, 142
Opposition. *See* Persecution

Parents. *See* Family
Pastor
   primary role of a, 91
   See also Leadership
Paton, John, his wife and baby's
   death, 138
Paul, flexibility of, 119-20
Persecution, ministry. *See* Ministry, opposition to
Preaching
   expository, 32
   lightweight, 32-34
   protective, 50-51
   purpose of, 32-34
Programs. *See* Evangelism

Risk. *See* Faith, great

Sacrifice, spirit of. *See* Giving
Scripture, studying, 57
Second Coming, anticipating
   the, 87-88
Sensitivity, in ministry. *See*
   Ministry
Service, Christian. *See* Ministry
Shepherd, man who knew the.
   See Twenty-third Psalm
Spartan, his desire to fight for
   his king, 131

Spencer, Edward W., doing his
   best, 128
Spiritual gifts, using one's, 19-
   20, 25
Submission, to church leadership. *See* Leadership
Sunday, worship on, 35

Teaching. *See* Preaching
Teamwork, in ministry. *See*
   Ministry
Thessalonian church, example
   of the, 75-93
Truett, George, 32
Twenty-third Psalm, recitation
   of, 101

Vision, a sense of, 115-19, 124-
   25
Visitation, 14-15

Watergate, 30
Women
   apparel of, 69-71
   preachers, 71
   responsibilities of, 69-72
Work
   behavior at, 68, 73
   of the ministry. *See* Ministry
Worship
   emphasis on, 40-41
   place of, 36
   times of, 35
Wuest, Kenneth, on 2 Corinthians 6:16, 46